EASTERN LIGHT

Smith, Steve. *Ways of Wisdom: Readings on the Good Life,* (University Press of America, 1983).

Smith, Steve. *Everyday Zen: Love and Work,* (HarperOne, 1989) Charlotte Joko Beck, editor.
———*Nothing Special: Living Zen* (1993), (HarperOne, 1989) Charlotte Joko Beck, editor.

Steve Smith has facilitated Quaker adult education courses and retreats in numerous settings, including Quaker Center (Ben Lomond, CA), Pendle Hill (Philadelphia, PA), Friends General Conference, and other Quaker gatherings in the United States.

EASTERN LIGHT

AWAKENING TO PRESENCE IN ZEN, QUAKERISM, AND CHRISTIANITY

Steve Smith

QUPublishing
Quaker Universalist Fellowship

Eastern Light, Awakening to Presence in Zen, Quakerism, and Christianity is published by QUPublishing, an Imprint of Quaker Universalist Fellowship <www.universalistfriends.org>.

Content compiled and written by Steve Smith
Permissions for all copyrighted reproduced text given to Steve Smith
Content editing by Steve Smith
Copy editing for print by Ellie Caldwell
Copy editing for eBook by William Rogan
Index for print book by Mary Klein, *Western Friend*
Cover and content layout and design by Lyn Cope
Print and eBook production arrangements and oversight by QUPublishing
Cover graphic: *An Ais Sunrise* by Lyn Cope

Titles and text are set in ITC Benguiat™ designed by Ed Benguiat for ITC, U.S. Benguiat is based on typefaces from the Art Nouveau period.
Header and endnotes are set in WarnockPro™ designed by Robert Slimbach for Adobe Originals, U.S. Patent Des. 454,152. Warnock Pro, a contemporary classic inspired by 18th century British Caslon and Baskerville fonts.
The decorative Seashell font created by Okaycat, a Japanese Company located in Vancouver, BC.

Print masters provided by QUPublications.
Print on demand by Lightning Source, Ingram Content Group.
Digital eBook formats by Publishgreen.com.

Cataloging-in-Publication Data
QUPublishing, fully owned by Quaker Universalist Fellowship 2013
    Religion
    Quaker, Society of Friends
    Includes Index

Copies and eBooks available through QUBookstore, Quaker Books of FGC, Pendle Hill Bookstore, Quaker Book Centre (GB), Friends Bookstore CA, e-bookstores, and multiple mainstream book providers.

Contact: www.UniversalistFriends.org.; Books@UniversalistFriends.org.

ISBN 978-1-941309-00-1 (print)
ISBN 978-1-941309-01-8 (eReader: MOBI)
ISBN 979-1-941309-02-5 (eReader: EPUB)

Live in the Life of God, and feel it.
—George Fox, Epistle 95 (1655)

CONTENTS

ACKNOWLEDGEMENTS

In the lengthy gestation and birthing of this book, I have been helped by many kindly literary midwives (female and male), whose thoughtful critiques made my labors far more fruitful than they might otherwise have been. Remaining flaws are my own responsibility. I thank John Cobb, Forrest Curo, Ken Dale, Linda Dunn, Michael Dunn, Judith Favor, David Jamieson, Bruce Jones, T. Canby Jones, Sallie King, Judy Leshefka, David Levering, Dennis MacDonald, Carl Magruder, Lois McAfee, Bob McCoy, David Mann, Penelope Mann, Marshall Massey, Donna McDaniel, William Moreman, George Owen, Stan Searl, Pat Smith, Walter Sullivan, Don Swearer, Ava Thomas, Jan Turner, Alan Wright, and Ruth Morris Yarrow. To others whose names may be omitted here—please know that I am grateful to you as well.

I thank the good folks at Quaker Universalist Fellowship, especially Larry Spears, whose early interest heartened me as I explored publishing possibilities, and Lyn Cope, whose masterful oversight brought into being the book that you now hold in your hands. In the final stages of production, Mary Klein brought her efficient and meticulous skills to the project—a great gift.

My deepest thanks go to my wife, Pat, who has faithfully anchored me throughout the many years of preparation of this book. My life and my work are immeasurably better because of her love and support.

Finally, I thank in advance all who choose the companionship of my words and the story of my journey as we seek together to awaken to the highest things. May we come to know ourselves and one another more deeply in that which is eternal.

INTRODUCTION

Awakening early, I rise and view a new day. Through my eastern windows, morning light slants across furniture and floor, casting pools of color upon my western wall. The room transforms in beauty—familiar, yet utterly changed. The world opens to me and I am again an infant, enraptured by a new creation.

The deepest needs are for the highest things. This book is a record of my hunger to know the highest things throughout my entire life, to awaken to the light that illumines all. In my darkest night, that light dawned from the East, reminding me of what I already knew, but had forgotten.

To rediscover what one already knows is the most intimate form of knowledge, like discovering in one's pocket a treasure that was seemingly lost forever. In minor matters it is: "Of course! I knew that!" In deeper matters of the heart, it is the prodigal son returning, the realization that one is loved without reservation exactly as one is. For most of my adult life I had sought another kind of knowledge—aloof, comprehensive, general, a view from above: the universe seen from everywhere and nowhere. I sought this God's-eye view in my chosen discipline of academic philosophy, secretly hoping that if I achieved such an Olympian vision, I would at last find peace for my restless heart. That endeavor proved fruitless. Worse, as I searched through barren fields of bloodless concepts and came upon yet more unanswered questions, I lost touch with my soul.

Yet as defined in Greek antiquity, philosophy—*philosophia*, love of wisdom—still evokes my reverence. Wisdom is truth that nourishes, enabling us to be of greater service to ourselves, to others, and to all of creation. Socrates remains a hero for me.

Two primary kinds of knowledge are marked in many languages by separate terms: propositional knowledge, knowing that something is the case; and knowledge with a direct object, knowing as direct familiarity: "I *know* Paris—or Josephine, or the taste of a mango." I had been seeking the former kind of knowledge; what I secretly yearned for was the latter. To seek only propositional knowledge is to bypass the intimacy of direct awareness, or to recast it in unrecognizable formulas, content in the illusion that one can acquire facts while remaining untouched. Intellectual inquiry is then a cover for emotional cowardice—a state that I know all too well. When I open to the intimacy of direct knowing, I make myself vulnerable to transformation.

Religious practice seeks to heal the breach between propositional knowledge and direct familiarity, to recover from the illusion of isolation and reawaken to the many ways we are bound up with others and with life itself. As *practice*, it exemplifies a third form of knowledge—acquired skill or praxis, knowing *how*: "Yes, I know how to play golf," or "She really knows how to connect with people." Karen Armstrong, a respected, widely-read contemporary historian of religion, writes, "Religion is a practical discipline that teaches us to discover new capacities of mind and heart."[1] She observes that religious practice has the power to open us to "a transcendent dimension of life that (is) not simply an external reality 'out there' but (is) identical with the deepest level of (our) being."[2]

Armstrong suggests that because of our misguided efforts to capture the truths of religion in fixed propositions, "We have not been doing our practice and have lost the 'knack' of religion."[3] My own journey from abstract philosophy to Zen practice confirms this suggestion. Zen highlights the importance of knowing *how*; it is the cultivation of subtle yet powerful tools for living everyday life. To engage in Zen is to be constantly reminded that successful living is less a matter of accumulating information than of cultivating skills, and growing into what Aristotle called practical wisdom.[4]

Buddhism and Quakerism

Had I known where to look and what misconceptions to shed, I might have found within my own Quaker and Christian origins the very resources that my sick soul required. For many years, however, I could not see past my prejudices to the riches within my reach. In Buddhism I found a rigorous practice that brought healing balm. That discovery in turn threw unexpected light upon what I had failed to find in the familiar religious fixtures of my childhood—treasures that lay unrecognized at the center of my heart.

Reawakening to intimate awareness of my world, cultivating skills for successful living—these have been Zen's most precious gifts to me. Cross-cultural affinities between Quakerism and Zen eased the way for this mutual illumination. Some of these affinities are obvious: stark plainness and simplicity, deep silence and open receptivity are featured in both Quaker silent worship and Zen meditation. Others show themselves only upon deeper examination of the teachings of both traditions. Bodhidharma, the legendary first patriarch of Zen Buddhism, is traditionally credited with the following summation of Zen teaching:

A special tradition outside the scriptures;
No dependence upon words and letters;
Direct pointing at the soul...
Seeing into one's own nature, and the attainment of
    Buddhahood.[5]

The fourth line refers to the experience of enlightenment (*satori, kensho*), often simply called "awakening." Such an experience reveals to us that we have been living in a dull and troubled trance, oblivious to the vivid beauty of the world. Dogen Zenji, the great medieval Japanese Soto Zen master (1200-1253 C.E.), writes, "To be enlightened is to be intimate with all things."[6]

More than a millennium after Bodhidharma, on the opposite side of the globe in 17th Century England, a feisty religious radical unknowingly echoed these themes. Of his great spiritual awakenings, George Fox (1624-1691) wrote, "This I saw in the pure openings of the Light without the help of any man, neither did I then know where to find it in the Scriptures; though afterwards, searching the Scriptures, I found it. For I saw in that Light and Spirit which was before Scripture was given forth, ..."[7] His world was reborn: "All things were new, and all the creation gave another smell unto me than before, beyond what words can utter. I knew nothing but pureness, and innocency, and righteousness... ."[8] Fox wrote that in his awakened state, he "observed a dullness and drowsy heaviness upon people, which I wondered at...and I told people they must come to witness death to that sleepy, heavy nature... that their minds and hearts might be on things above."[9] Fox did not come to these insights through ruminating upon religious teachings, but through courageous, unblinking surrender to the actual condition of his own life. He called such surrender "standing still in the Light." This was the core of his spiritual practice, from which all of his ministry flows. Fox unknowingly echoed Zen: "No dependence upon words and letters." "Direct pointing at the soul."

To suggest that George Fox was a 17th Century English version of Bodhidharma would be a clumsy theological anachronism. Each man must be understood first within his own historical, cultural, and religious context. That said, the two figures display intriguing similarities. In paintings, Bodhidharma is typically depicted as a beetle-browed man of fierce, rough-hewn intensity. In later centuries, legends accumulated around him: "He fearlessly asserted the futility of building Buddhist

temples and of the recitation of the sutras... . For nine years
(he) remained seated before the wall of a monastery... . (He)
is said to have miraculously foiled his enemies' attempts to
poison him... ."[10] Is it a coincidence that George Fox—another
rough-hewn, singular figure, the man in leather breeches—often
denounced the "steeplehouses" of his time (declaring that "God
did not live in temples made with hands"[11]) or that by his own
account, he was the target of numerous failed attempts upon his
life, often making providential escapes from the clutches of his
opponents? Like graphic depictions of Bodhidharma's eyes, the
discerning fierceness of Fox's scrutiny of others was unnerving,
provoking frightened responses: "Don't pierce me so with thy
eyes! Keep thy eyes off me!"[12] Like Bodhidharma, Fox pursued
spiritual awakening with extraordinary intensity; he reports that
in his early years of seeking, "I fasted much, and walked abroad
in solitary places many days, and often took my Bible and went
and sat in hollow trees and lonesome places till night came on;
and frequently in the night walked mournfully about by myself,
for I was a man of sorrows in the times of the first workings of
the Lord in me."[13] William Penn noted the utter uniqueness of
Fox: "He was an original, being no man's copy."[14] The religious
genius of both Bodhidharma and Fox drove them toward spiritual
awakening, without concern for personal comfort and safety.

Both Zen and Quakerism lay claim to being distillations of
the experiential core of their respective traditions, Buddhism and
Christianity. (William Penn wrote a pamphlet about Quakerism
titled "Primitive Christianity Revived."[15]) Both traditions abandon
doctrinal definitions in favor of religious practices whose
purpose is to awaken us to Presence in this very moment. Both
point to a theological paradox hidden within our everyday delusions: we are *always* immersed in Sacred Reality—yet we remain
blind to it. The classic 8th Century Buddhist poem, *Sandokai*
(commonly translated as "The Identity of Relative and Absolute")
contains these lines: "Reading words you should grasp the great

reality... . If you do not see the Way, you do not see it even as you walk upon it."[16] Zen masters employ a startling array of means to cut through the obscuring thickets of words, in order to shock their students into an immediate realization of "the great reality."[17]

The ubiquity of Divine Presence is repeatedly affirmed in Judeo-Christian scripture. Moses declares (Deut. 30:14) that "The word is very near to you: it is in your mouth and in your heart... ." The psalmist asks,

> Where can I go from your spirit? Or where can I flee from your presence?
> If I ascend to heaven, you are there; if I make my bed in Sheol, you are there.
> If I take the wings of the morning and settle at the farthest limits of the sea, even there your hand shall lead me, and your right hand shall hold me fast.
> (Psalm 139:7-10)

Jesus assures his disciples that "I am with you always, to the end of the age." (Matt. 28:20) St. Paul agrees with a pagan poet that in God, "we live, and move, and have our being." (Acts 17:28) and reaffirms Moses' words, quoted above. (Romans10:8)

Although we are always immersed in Mystery, we live as if we were separate from it. Isaac Penington (1616-1679), a Quaker mystic and contemporary of George Fox who endured lengthy imprisonment for his refusal to abandon his religious convictions, put this paradox sharply:

> But is it not strange, that thou shouldst be of it, and not be able to know and own it, in this day of its manifestation; but call the light which is spiritual and eternal (and gives the true and certain knowledge of Christ) natural? What! Of God, of Christ, (having received the Spirit, the living well) and yet not know the mystery of life within, nor its pure voice in this present day! But limit the unlimited One to a form of words formerly spoken by him![18]

When Sacred Reality becomes a mere idea rather than Living Presence, we have lost our way. Concepts and words that should point beyond themselves assume a false reality of their own, limiting and even replacing that to which they refer—a category mistake that the philosopher Alfred North Whitehead called the fallacy of misplaced concreteness.[19] The opening words of the *Tao Te Ching* declare, "The Tao which can be spoken of is not the eternal Tao."[20]

A traditional Zen saying is, "You may use your finger to point at the moon—but do not mistake the finger for the moon." When we view the moon with an open body and mind, we awaken to wonder and reverence, giving joyful expression to our experience. Eager to share with others, we try to capture the ineffable in words, using the tools that are familiar to us: symbols, metaphors, and rituals of our own tradition. For Bodhidharma and Dogen, that tradition was the Buddhism of their time and place; for George Fox, it was Christianity in 17th Century England. Yet for us, the spiritual power of their vision rests not in those outward forms, but in our intuitive intimation of the Mystery to which they point. As Paul Knitter writes, "Christian language, like all religious language, is, in its entire vocabulary, made up of fingers pointing to the moon."[21]

The Primacy of Practice

When I stand some distance away from you, I may not be able to discern where you are pointing, nor comprehend why what you see evokes such wonder and zeal; only when I realize that my own standpoint is but one among many, may I begin to appreciate your perspective. Likewise, ministry that does not speak to one person may be exactly what another seeker needs to receive. A similar humility is required of us as we survey the immense variety and protean power of spiritual insights in countless cultural settings.

Yet how shall we make room for this seemingly laudable latitude regarding religious symbols without descending to a "lowest common denominator," thereby arriving at tasteless spiritual pablum? As a boy I heard this question posed by elderly Quakers who were concerned about the decline of their beloved Society—usually accompanied by plaintive recitation of Matthew 5:13 (KJV): "Ye are the salt of the earth: but if the salt have lost his savour, wherewith shall it be salted? It is thenceforth good for nothing, but to be cast out, and to be trodden under the foot of men."

In my experience, generous respect for other religions is best grounded in deep fidelity to our own authentic religious practice. When I try to explain to others how I reconcile Zen practice with my Quaker and Christian identity, I am of two minds. If I compare theologies, lining up Buddhism and Christianity in order to read off similarities and contrasts, I fumble; my efforts to explain myself become forced and unpersuasive. Yet in my personal spiritual life, Buddhism, Quakerism, and Christianity meld seamlessly into my own singular journey. The beloved contemporary Buddhist teacher, Jack Kornfield, relates this story: "One young woman who had become very involved in Buddhist practice returned to her parents' home. She struggled with their Christian Fundamentalism for a time, until she sorted things out. Then she sent a letter back to the monastery stating, 'My parents hate me when I'm a Buddhist, but they love me when I'm a Buddha.'"[22]

A fellow graduate student in philosophy once told me that his strategy in winning a philosophical argument was "Distinguish and conquer." He was very skilled at doing this. Was it mere coincidence that his wife (also a graduate student in philosophy) seemed unhappy in the marriage? Buddhist teachings—and indeed, mysticism in all of its forms—observe that exclusive reliance upon discursive reasoning highlights differences, promoting division and discord. In contrast, when we return to the infinite depth and breadth of this moment, we rediscover our underlying connections with others and with all of life. Purely theoretical puzzles disappear or become irrelevant; as the Buddha delicately observed, they reveal themselves to be "questions that tend not to edification."[23]

A corollary of this spiritual insight is the paradox that we draw closer to one another to the degree that we become more fully ourselves. Thus I do not offer my reflections in this book as a spiritual map for others to follow. There is no "one size fits all" spirituality or religious identity; the shape of soul-making is unique to each individual. The Buddha's final words were, "Be a lamp unto yourself"—that is, learn to recognize and commit to your own deepest insights. Again, George Fox unknowingly echoed this directive. Margaret Fell (1614-1702), the spiritual mother of Quakerism and the eventual wife of Fox, relates the moment when his ministry "cut me to the heart": confronting a cleric who drew upon scripture to refute his challenges, Fox declared, "You will say, Christ saith this, and the Apostles say this; but what canst thou say? Art thou a Child of Light, and hast walked in the Light, and what thou speakest, is it inwardly from God?"[24] I am of greatest service to others when I am true to myself: honest testimony from my own path proves to be more helpful than presuming to know what others should do.

God-Talk

The only real voyage of discovery...consists not in seeking new landscapes but in having new eyes.

—Marcel Proust[25]

My childhood home was suffused with a distinctively Quaker vision of Christianity, centering upon the spiritual and moral teachings of Jesus—especially the Sermon on the Mount. These teachings became etched upon my heart. Yet the conventional theological language in which they were couched gradually lost its power over my mind, replaced by intellectual skepticism and aimless spiritual longing. Zen practice became a new wineskin for that longing, refocusing my spiritual energies and freeing my use of Christian and Quaker language from the straitjacket of literalism. I count as one of Zen's greatest gifts that it has restored to me the evocative power of Judeo-Christian scripture.

When I think of God, I do not picture to myself a disembodied, supreme Intelligence who can be persuaded by human supplication to intervene in the natural course of events. In the minds of many orthodox Christians, this admission will brand me as a non-theist or even an atheist. I choose not to invest energy in rebutting this charge. In my personal lexicon, the term "God" and its cognates hint at a Reality that is beyond the power of words to capture, a vast and potent Mystery.[26]

Friends affirm that this Divine Reality is found within every human breast—that there is "that of God in every one."[27] Awakening to this Presence, we "come to know the hidden unity in the Eternal Being"[28]—our essential interconnection with one another and with all creation. Zen makes similar claims regarding "Buddha-Nature," an empowering awareness to which we awaken through disciplined spiritual practice, revealing the truth of "Interbeing."[29] I hesitate to suggest that these phrases—"that of God in every one" and "Buddha-Nature"—refer to the same underlying reality. In view of the unique historical tapestries of Buddhism and Christianity, such a cross-cultural equation is dubious. Yet I personally find these phrases equally satisfactory in pointing to my own inner experience.

Because of fond memories of my childhood religious instruction, I continue to use some traditional Christian terminology. Yet I dissociate myself from the intolerance and exclusivity that often accompany this language. I invite readers for whom my Christian words and scriptural citations carry negative baggage to translate them into symbols that evoke their own spiritual insights. A guiding thread of theological reconstruction in these pages is to reclaim—for myself, and possibly for others—the power of Christian language, even as I respect, admire, and draw upon other great religious traditions.

The following chapters are linked by a common theme, the insights that arise as we awaken to the reality of the present moment. Breaking free of the conceptual cocoon that insulates us from our lives, coming to our senses, we discover that what Jesus called "the Kingdom of God" is indeed among and within us. (Luke 17:21) Moments of awakening are not always blissful or reassuring; they can be disconcerting, even devastating. Others are quiet reminders of who and where we are, small epiphanies that reorient us to what is most important. Their meaning may be lost on us in the moment that they occur, to be realized later in what the English poet, Wordsworth, called "emotion recollected in tranquility."[30]

Scattered through these pages are accounts of such pivotal moments in my life—personal parables, intense experiences that have shaped my perspective and directed my steps into the future. Some were traumatic, others uplifting. *For emphasis, I highlight these accounts by the typographical convention of italics.*

Unless otherwise noted, all quotations from the Old and New Testaments of the Christian Bible are from the New Revised Standard Version.

Chapters are organized according to the traditional stages of the mystic's path: *purgation* (dropping all denial and self-deception, facing one's brokenness and shadow self); *illumination* (out of such radical self-honesty spring moments of grace and insight); and *union* (the gladness of awakening to our intrinsic bond with all of creation).

Part I: Purgation

CHAPTER ONE: **A Quaker In the Zendo** relates the journey from my childhood in an Iowa Quaker farm family, through anxious years of academic striving that imploded into humiliating personal crisis—and to recovery through years of psychotherapy and Zen practice, returning me to a renewed engagement with my Quaker roots.

CHAPTER TWO: **Standing Still In the Light** draws upon the records of Quakerism, writings of George Fox and other early Friends, where I find—to my wonder and delight—explicit guidelines for spiritual practice that are often overlooked by Friends today. I spell out these guidelines in experiential terms.

CHAPTER THREE: **Pure Passion** expands upon the theme of Chapter Two, linking the spiritual practice of "standing still in the Light" to an understanding of psychotherapy, meditation, and the Passion of Christ. Again my account is personal, building upon my own experience.

Part II: Illumination

CHAPTER FOUR: **Living Peace** details my efforts to understand the Peace Testimony of early Friends. I find it to be not (as is commonly supposed) the endorsement of a sweeping philosophical principle of pacifism, but rather, the outcome of disciplined spiritual practice. When we stand in utter sincerity in the Light, the causes of violence and hatred melt away, bringing us into sweet harmony with all of creation.

CHAPTER FIVE: **Healing Gender Hurt** explores the meaning of the Peace Testimony for gender conflict—especially what is often called "the war of the sexes." I explore the meaning of masculinity in the light of Friends' Peace Testimony. I share my own efforts to heal and to foster the healing of others.

CHAPTER SIX: **Friendly Pedagogy** traces the spiritual roots that nourish Quaker schools and suggests that the distinctive ethos of such schools derives from Friends' unique manner of conducting meetings for business. I tease out implications of Friends' spirituality for humane, effective teaching.

Part III: Union

CHAPTER SEVEN: **In the Love of Nature** draws from my childhood on an Iowa farm. In this chapter, I probe the contributions of Quaker spirituality to an overriding challenge of our time, the gathering storm of global climate change and environmental decay. We cannot hope to restore the earth while we ourselves remain alienated from her.

CHAPTER EIGHT: **Joyful Service** argues that the work of peace and justice—"mending the world"—is most effective when it is motivated not by indignation, fear, or anger, but by the transforming, reconciling power of hearts that have surrendered into the crucible of the Light. Reactive emotions may be necessary in order to cut through our complacence—but only love can overcome hatred and promote true justice.

CHAPTER NINE: **Walking Cheerfully** unites the themes of the previous chapters in a vision of reconciliation and redemption in *this* life—living "the Kingdom of God" in a broken world. If the deepest needs are for the highest things, what is highest can be found here and now, in this very life—if we have eyes to see.

While I draw upon fine scholarship from many sources, I do not write as a scholar addressing other scholars, but rather as an earnest seeker, sharing my brokenness, my failures, and my modest insights in the hope that my readers may find their way along their own paths to healing and wholeness, whatever those paths may be. In that spirit I write not only for those who self-identify as Quakers or Buddhists—but for all who yearn for the highest things.

Awakening to our own deepest springs of wisdom promises more than we can now dream or imagine. In the final lines of *Walden*, Henry David Thoreau writes, "Only that day dawns to which we are awake. There is more day to dawn. The sun is but a morning star."[31] His words are a departure point for the following pages. May the morning star—eastern light—reveal the true light, which enlightens everyone.

Part I:

PURGATION

CHAPTER ONE

A QUAKER
IN THE ZENDO

Early one April morning in 1981, I arise quietly in my rented home in Honolulu, don casual, loose-fitting clothing, then slip outside and stroll down moist streets under spreading mango trees to the small Zen center nearby. In Hawaii for a sabbatical leave to study Asian philosophy and religion, I have found that my temporary home is thabut five minutes' walk from a Zendo.

*On that April morning, I begin formal Zen practice at Koko An Diamond Sangha. Each weekday for two months I sit with other Zen students for an hour, broken by a few minutes of silent walking meditation. With legs folded on a black **zafu** and zabuton, I sit bolt upright facing the wall, following my breath, returning my attention again and again to the present moment. Bells mark the beginning and end of each sitting period. The scent of burning incense wafts from an altar. A senior student sometimes slowly stalks the room with the traditional **kyosaku**, a flattened stick used to deliver a bracing yet painless whack to the shoulders of a sleepy*

17

or inattentive meditator, after which both striker and strikee gravely bow.

Removed many years and thousands of miles from the Iowa Quaker farm family into which I was born, I feel awkward and vaguely embarrassed, afraid of behaving inappropriately. Yet my venture into Zen practice is no mere sampling of the exotic to adorn an otherwise purely intellectual interest. I am not making a tourist's tour of the Orient; rather, I am dead serious, motivated by a desperate yearning to heal from my troubled and broken past.

Driven by unrelenting self-expectations, I had climbed an apparently ascending path through college and graduate school into my first full-time teaching appointment and marriage. Each success, each award and public recognition brought private depression in its wake, however, as I once again discovered that the peace of mind and self-acceptance I craved could not be earned by excelling in the course of learning I had chosen to pursue.

I knew no other way. Traditional claims of Western theism seemed implausible to me. Years of academic skepticism had corroded the naïve faith of my childhood; I trusted only my intellect. For years I had called myself "an open-minded atheist," not ready to close the door on faith, yet unable to believe. But my skepticism was unwilling: secretly, I doubted my doubts. For in my bones still lingered hints of the awe and wonder that I had felt as a child upon first hearing the stories of the Bible: the poetic grandeur of the Old Testament, the astonishing power of the life and teachings of Jesus. Like a delicate plant locked in the dark, my inchoate longings were aimless, diverted into the elaborate byways of analytic philosophy, which tantalized but never satisfied. My head was stranger to my heart.

The pain arising from that internal divorce led me down dark paths of self-abuse. Even as I established myself at a small college in Southern California, was married to a talented and beautiful woman, saw the birth of our son, gained tenure, and published my dissertation, my private life was rapidly deteriorating. This decline showed itself above all in my escalating misuse of alcohol. Though they were entirely absent from my childhood, during a year of study in Germany in 1959-60 I had discovered the charms of fine wine and beer. Later, as a resident tutor in a Harvard house, I warmed to the elegant gentility of expensive sherry and carefully mixed martinis. Upon arriving in Southern California, I quickly acquired a liquor cabinet of only the finest brands; and in the first year or two of my marriage, my wife and I enjoyed regular cocktails on weekend evenings. But as pressures mounted in my new career and my expanding roles as husband and father, my use of alcohol increasingly obeyed an insidious master that seemed beyond my rational control. Instead of a drink or two to enliven sharing around a good meal, alcohol gradually became the centerpiece of my week, excluding other more convivial, sociable activities. If the effects of a couple of drinks seemed desirable, several more would surely be better. Any internal mechanism I once had to alert me that "This is enough—stop here!" was drowned out by my stronger compulsion for release and oblivion.

Thanksgiving 1973: we are to spend the day with friends in Orange County. Knowing that alcohol will be freely available in the home of our hosts, I decide to get an early start—and surreptitiously down a few swigs of vodka before we depart. Driving down the winding mountain road with my wife and son, I recognize that I am already too drunk to drive safely. I pull over and ask my wife to take the wheel. Arriving at our destination, I pick up my drinking where I had left off. Sometime that afternoon, even as I remain sociably engaged with others, I slip into a blackout—meaning that the next day, I do not remember anything about the remaining hours of our visit. As I awaken that Friday morning to my accustomed hangover, my wife tells me that in a moment of drunken clumsiness the previous evening, I had dropped my 20-month-old son. (He was frightened but not hurt.)

I am overcome with shame. I resolve to make an appointment to talk with my doctor early in the coming week and decide to abstain from any use of alcohol until that time. I sustain that pledge to myself through what in AA is called "white-knuckle sobriety"—a fiercely willed refusal to yield to the cravings that cry out from every cell of my body. When I finally see the doctor, he tells me simply that I must stop drinking altogether. I get myself into psychotherapy. In January 1974 I fall off the wagon briefly, until my therapist helps me to see what I am doing—and I return to sobriety. My recovery continues to the present day.

This recovery was uneven, however, marked by a detour through another form of substance abuse: marijuana. Once when I was a boy my father had casually pointed out marijuana plants growing as weeds on our farm. As a graduate student in the '60s, I had experimented with pot; and now, though I had put the use of alcohol behind me, I returned to clandestine use of marijuana to explore alternate modes of consciousness. My illegal activities were frightening to my wife, who was employed at a college in the same small town as I was. Despite her distress I persisted in my private pursuit, rationalizing my use in various ways. Being high seemed to free me from old, rigid and confining patterns of consciousness, showing me more beautiful, joyful ways of being in the world. Yet physical and emotional costs mounted as well: increased susceptibility to illness, emotional isolation augmented by my solitary obsession, a flatness of affect and energy following each use—and finally, deepening depression, plunging me into yet another round of intensive therapy. If the siren call of chemically altered consciousness had lured me along enticing paths of self-discovery, that call in the end drew me downward rather than upward toward the light. Over time, I weaned myself from this dependence as well. I also terminated a 10-year habit of cigarette smoking and lost some 30 excessive pounds. Counseling and other personal growth activities were important aids in my prolonged efforts to heal.

Meanwhile, I was transforming my understanding of my chosen academic pursuit. Philosophy (the term means "love of wisdom") once encompassed the inquiry into how to live rightly and well; thus I reflected that I might find resources in my own discipline to reorder my life into a healthier balance. My hope would not be realized through the kind of philosophy that was featured in my graduate training, however. Technical and precise, obsessed with the analysis of language, and distrustful of larger questions of meaning and value, it had proved to be more an agent of my decline than an avenue of recovery. I widened my vision of philosophy, sampling traditions that had been neglected in my undergraduate and graduate training. Responding to student interest and to my own needs, I created a new course ("Theories of the Good Life"[1]) that explored various views of happiness and well being. This exploration led me not only to treasures of the West that are commonly ignored in analytic philosophy, including stoicism, Epicureanism, scripture, mysticism, literature, and psychology, but also for the first time to the extraordinary philosophical and religious traditions of the East.

Ten years of formal academic training in philosophy had not introduced me to Asian thought. I began to rectify that deficiency with more accessible materials from India and East Asia, writings intended primarily for Western readers.[2] Their reports of transforming spiritual experience seemed credible to me. With dawning excitement, I recognized the experiences reported in these writings, discerning forgotten truths that reemerged slowly out of the mists of my rootless rational trance. For several years, I was content to read hungrily and to record my ruminations in a personal journal. Portions of my readings found their way into my courses, where I could expound on my limited understanding. Eventually, however, this piecemeal remedial study was not enough; I craved more authoritative training and experience. Providentially, a sabbatical leave loomed—and I chose to spend it with my family at what was perhaps the most propitious site in the world for the study of comparative philosophy, the intellectual meeting of West and East: the University of Hawaii in Manoa, Honolulu.

Thus in April 1981 I found myself strolling down those moist morning streets to the Zendo on Kaloa Way, embarking upon an odyssey through a tradition far removed from my own, toward myself and my own roots.

My first encounters with Zen meditation were intriguing and suggestive. Grounded in a tradition older than Christianity, Buddhist meditation had evolved over many centuries of trial and error into a simplified, experientially refined form. I immediately found it helpful—clarifying, steadying, softening the edges of my life. Wishing to continue my fledgling practice upon returning to the mainland, I sought the advice of the resident Zen master at Koko An, Robert Aitken Roshi. He advised me to visit the Zen Center of Los Angeles (ZCLA), a thriving spiritual community presided over by Maezumi Roshi, a Japanese teacher with extensive experience with Western students. In August 1981 I participated in an intensive seven-day meditation retreat (called a *sesshin*) at ZCLA. This week was a revelation to me. Through a painful but promising ordeal of zazen, I gained insight into the potential of this seemingly exotic discipline. I was assigned to work with a resident teacher, Charlotte Joko Beck, an American-born woman who had come late to Zen after having raised four children largely on her own. Her down-to-earth, no-nonsense directness, her compassionate understanding of my struggles, and her intuitive gifts in supporting my efforts to learn cemented the foundation for my long-term commitment to Zen practice.

Since 1981 I have maintained a daily meditation regimen, and for some 15 years augmented that daily practice by occasional retreats lasting from two to seven days. In 1985 I undertook the project of editing Joko's talks on Zen, revising rough verbatim transcripts into publishable form.[3] My editorial labors provided rich learning: as I sought language that directly and faithfully expressed Joko's thought, I made it my own as well.

My growing immersion in Zen was fraught with pain, however. Long-standing issues in my marriage finally came to a head, and my wife withdrew from it and from me. Though I was devastated by our separation and subsequent divorce, I later came to accept it as a necessary ending, releasing each of us for new lives. Throughout this prolonged agony, daily *zazen* helped to keep me sane.

During several years of single fatherhood followed by a new, fulfilling marriage, Zen meditation has become a mainstay of my spiritual practice. I credit it with an incremental yet thoroughgoing transformation of my life. As I uncover and face underlying fears, space opens for love—and I find greater equanimity, steadiness, and peace. Knowing myself better, I forget myself more easily and release into the flow of life. Less self-preoccupied, more able to listen to others, I am a better father, husband, teacher, and friend. I struggle less, yet accomplish more. Though certainly not without pain, my life is easier, more natural and expansive. Entries in my personal journal chronicle this unfolding process: "Something is happening to my body and brain, bit by bit, that feels right and healthy." (August 1986) "Zazen is marvelous. It returns me to myself, and to the unspeakable beauty at the heart of all things." (September 1986) "I increasingly sense an underpinning of joy, as I awaken to grounding in what I call 'Blessed Awareness,' a sweet, imperturbable, infinite space within which all is lovingly encompassed." (May 1996)

My cumulative experience with Zen practice confirms its rightness for me, beyond any serious doubt. I expect to continue it for as long as I am able. Yet I remain detached from outward forms of Buddhist ritual. Out of deference and respect for the tradition, when attending retreats at the Zen Center I participated in religious observances: chants, bows, formal oryoki (eating) practice, and so on. These manifestations of Japanese Soto Zen felt alien to me, however; they did not express my own authentic religious impulses.

Indeed, over years of my expanding investment in Zen, a curious paradox has emerged: the more thoroughly I give myself to zazen, the more authentically Quaker I become. When I began Zen practice in 1981, my connection to the Religious Society of Friends was tenuous, sustained more by nostalgia and cultural familiarity than by deep commitment. The radical openness of zazen has opened me to my own religious identity, however, and I find that identity to be clear—I am a Friend.

I find confirmation of my experience in the writings of one who has traveled a similar path: Father Robert Kennedy, a Jesuit priest who, while remaining within the Catholic tradition, has taken Buddhist vows as an authorized Zen master. He writes that "Zen Buddhism need not be looked at as a religion at all, but as a way of seeing life that can enhance any religious faith,"[4] and adds that "I personally have experienced that the practice of Zen, under the guidance of a teacher, can be integrated into the Christian life; it can deepen Christian prayer and root our faith not just in our head but in our whole person."[5]

An analogy from my youth helps me to understand this paradox. As a naïve mid-western college student, I spent a year of undergraduate study in Germany. Immersion in a foreign culture brought a wealth of information about Europe and the globe; yet my chief insights concerned my country of origin. Viewing the United States from across an ocean, I came to grasp as never before what it means to be an American. While I reveled in my European sojourn and through it was able to see more clearly many flaws of the United States, on balance my view from afar reaffirmed my national identity and strengthened the love of my native land. Likewise, years of intensive Zen practice have confirmed how deeply rooted I am in the Religious Society of Friends. By a curious cross-cultural alchemy, Zen has reawakened me to the spiritual riches of Quakerism and Christianity.

In his monumental study, *The Varieties of Religious Experience*, psychologist-philosopher William James draws upon a distinction between two kinds of believers: the once-born and the twice-born.[6] The former are naturally happy, well-adjusted souls whose disposition is cheerful, upbeat, accepting of their place and prospects. They find no reason to question the tradition in which they were raised. In contrast, the twice-born doubt themselves and their received values. They struggle against the felt inadequacy of their lives, spend years in the wilderness, and finally break through to reconciliation and healing joy. The biblical stories of the prodigal son and the lost sheep, Homer's *Odyssey*, and many other mythic journeys are variants of this archetypal theme.

Certainly not once-born, I have searched and struggled to find my way home. But if what I sought was already at hand, why did I not simply reach out and clasp it gladly to my heart? An ancient story tells of a poor man who searched far and wide for a rich treasure. Finally, a sage in a distant land told him that he would find what he sought in his own home. He returned—and uncovered a life-transforming treasure in his own hearth.

In rediscovering through Buddhism the power of my own religious origins, I find that I am not alone. In a compelling volume of personal spiritual journeys, *Beside Still Waters: Jews, Christians, and the Way of the Buddha*, author after author testifies to a renewed appreciation for his or her own religious tradition through a personal encounter with Buddhism. As one author, Rabbi Zalman Schachter-Shalomi, declares, "What is so wonderful is that once...you go back to your own literature, you see that it's there in the faith of the religion of origin. It's been there all along! But it's almost as if the scales fell off the eyes because we went next door."[7] My searching "next door" has also been a revelation. If I had not undertaken my travels, I might never have discovered the treasure I already possessed and might well have remained quietly desperate.

Each path is unique. Although Zen practice has been for me a great blessing, I do not urge others to follow in my footsteps. I am no closet evangelical Buddhist among Friends, nor do I offer exotic oriental trinkets to adorn the plain mantel of Quakerism. Whether Quaker and Buddhist spirituality are at their core indistinguishable, I cannot say. Rather, my Zen journey has helped me to appreciate features of Quaker spiritual practice that I had formerly overlooked.

Radically understood and faithfully followed, the Society of Friends needs no bolstering by alien traditions; rather, Quakerism is itself a fully sufficient path of transforming power and grace. If contemporary Friends' faith and practice seem to lack inspiration and vision, that shortfall stems not from an inherent deficiency within Quakerism itself—but because we have forgotten our way to the Source from which early Friends drew their strength. Yearning to grow in the Light, we can find what we need within the tradition of George Fox and Margaret Fell, William Penn and John Woolman, Elizabeth Fry and Lucretia Mott.

Returning to Quakerism, I do not leave my travels behind but bring them with me. Always will I see the Religious Society of Friends both from within and without, as one who was born into its traditions yet explores it anew, a native speaker who is learning its language for the first time. I am glad to be both citizen and alien, native and newcomer—a Quaker in the Zendo.

CHAPTER TWO

STANDING STILL IN THE LIGHT

*Returning with new eyes to my own Quaker hearth,
I read in Fox's Journal and epistles, the writings of
Isaac Penington and early Quaker women, and recent
scholars on Quaker history. I am startled by treasures
of insight that give practical guidance in finding one's
way to the Light. Buried within the ashes of my life,
long hidden while I elsewhere earnestly sought solace
and now revealing itself to my wondering mind, I
awaken to the gift of my own heart—floating in the
mind of God.*

Be Still and Cool

In 1658, Lady Elizabeth Claypole—beloved daughter of Oliver Cromwell, the "Lord Protector of England"—is "very sick and troubled in mind, and nothing could comfort her." Cromwell is under threat of assassination, sharpening Elizabeth's mental distress. Elizabeth will die in August, to be joined in death

27

one month later by her father. The leader of the rapidly-growing Quaker movement has gained a reputation as a keen discerner of spirits and a worker of miraculous healings. Hearing of Elizabeth's sickly condition, Fox is "moved of the Lord to write a paper and send it to her to be read unto her." His letter to Claypole provides intimate insight into the causes of spiritual distress and how they may be eased:

> Be still and cool in thy own mind and spirit from thy own thoughts, and then thou wilt feel the principle of God to turn thy mind to the Lord God, whereby thou wilt receive his strength and power from whence life comes, to allay all tempests, against blusterings and storms. That it is which moulds up into patience, into innocency, into soberness, into stillness, into stayedness, into quietness, up to God, with his power... which keeps peace, and brings up the witness in thee... When thou art in the transgression of the life of God in the particular, the mind flies up in the air, and the creature is led into the night, and nature goes out of his course... and so it comes to be all of a fire... .

> Therefore be still a while from thy own thoughts, searching, seeking, desires and imaginations, and be stayed in the principle of God in thee...; and thou wilt find strength from him and find him to be a present help in time of trouble, in need, and to be a God at hand. ...There thou wilt come to receive and feel the physician of value, which clothes people in their right mind, whereby they may serve God and do his will... . What the light doth make manifest and discover, temptations, confusions, distractions, distempers; do not look at the temptations, confusions, corruptions, but at the light that discovers them, that makes them manifest; and with the same light you will feel over them, (you will) receive power to stand against them. ... For looking down at sin, and corruption, and distraction, you are swallowed up in it; but looking at the light that discovers them, you will see over them. That will give victory;

and you will find grace and strength; and there is the first step of peace.[1]

Fox's words are a primer for the practice of silent Quaker worship. Though they did not save Lady Claypole from an early death, they are a balm to my troubled heart. In rough-hewn 17th-Century prose, Fox offers an apt diagnosis not only of Lady Claypole's condition, but of mine as well. Effective healing begins with careful diagnosis—and when the malady has spiritual roots, an accurate diagnosis requires larger insight than can be discerned by the small mind. To see clearly, I must awaken to a searching light that lays bare all confusion and error. This same light enfolds me in a healing embrace—and I gain strength to move forward.

Fox ascribes this vaster vision without hesitation to "the Lord God"—yet for him (and for us today) religious names and theological descriptions are less important than the dynamics of the inner process, recognized in many religions and variously clothed in their distinctive language, symbols, and rituals. Fox invokes "the witness" or observing self—a central feature in awakening to presence.[2]

Isaac Penington, a 17th-Century Quaker mystic, offers another paradigmatic account:

> Be no more than God hath made thee. Give over thine own willing; give over thine own running; give over thine own desire to know or to be any thing, and sink down to the seed which God sows in thy heart, and let that grow in thee, and be in thee, and breathe in thee, and act in thee, and thou shalt find by sweet experience that the Lord knows that, and loves and owns that, and will lead it to the inheritance of life, which is his portion.[3]

Diagnosis

According to long-standing Christian doctrine, the greatest human sin is pride. To paraphrase Penington, it is trying to be more than God has made—living in self-deception and hypocrisy. Such pretense often stems from a hidden fear than I am "not enough"; that I lack some fundamental feature of full humanity. If this were true, then the present moment with all of its uncertainty and messy imperfection would be intolerable—for to plumb it would be to face my failure as a human being. To avoid facing this intolerable thought, I hold my uneasiness at bay with an infinite variety of compensatory behaviors.

Yet to run from the present moment is to flee the only place where true healing and comfort may be found. Fox describes this fleeing journey in graphic terms: "When thou art in the transgression of the life of God in the particular, the mind flies up in the air, and the creature (i.e. one's physical being) is led into the night, and nature goes out of his course... . (And) so it comes to be all of a fire... ." God is here, now, in the particular—the details of my life. When I pursue temptations or obsess about my fears, my mind flies up in the air and I am led into the night. To find the life of God in the particular, I must surrender fully to this moment and bear my own pain, without fleeing or flailing.

Seeing the darkness into which I have wandered— alcoholism and drug abuse, alienation from myself— brings humiliation and shame. Even those who love me cannot walk with me into my anguish, nor remove its sting. Still, my willingness to take that walk owes something to the lessons of my Quaker childhood. Once when I am small, in an unguarded moment my mother tells me that for all of his flaws, my father is honest with himself. I am deeply impressed, admiring his courage. A good Quaker man, my father had in some measure lived into a central feature of Friends' spiritual practice—severe submission to the truth of one's life.

Fox came to his own great 1647 opening through just such devastating surrender: he writes, "when all my hopes... in all men were gone, so that I had nothing outwardly to help me, nor could tell what to do, then, Oh then, I heard a voice which said, 'There is one, even Christ Jesus, that can speak to thy condition', and when I heard it my heart did leap for joy."[4]

An Annihilating Path

Perhaps every major religious tradition calls for death of the small self so that we may open upon ultimate Reality. Early Friends' understanding of this death was trenchant. A leading Quaker scholar, Douglas Gwyn, describes the spirituality of early Friends as a "harrowing, annihilating path,"[5] a "spirituality of desolation."[6] He writes that "Quaker preachers offered not sublime mystical transport but a traumatic passage through death to a realm where God's will is known first-hand and power to obey is received."[7] This is the narrow gate, the way to the kingdom. "The desolation of the self must take place on the inner landscape before one comes to know the Christ returned."[8]

The harrowing, annihilating path that was followed by Fox and other early Friends requires extraordinary commitment and faith, a willingness to risk all of myself. Can I surrender so completely? Such a commitment is required if I am to emerge through the door of Quakerism into a rich spiritual life.

Discipline

Like others, I want my religion to be easy, comfortable, undemanding; I have too much to do already, too many claims upon my time and energy. I want a soothing sideline to occupy some of my leisure time when I am so inclined. From time to time, I busy myself with Quaker activities, but shrink from changing my life. This tepid attitude is remote from the terrifying yet exhilarating call of authentic Christianity and Quakerism, indeed from devout religious practice in any tradition. Even after devastating crisis had led me to explore Asian traditions, my everyday life was scarcely changed. I read, I ruminated, I enthused, I wrote—yet went on with my life much as before.

31

A providential coincidence nudged me from appreciative specta-tor to active participant—the presence of a Zen center just five minutes' walk from my new home.

Since that change, I have become keenly aware of a water-shed in spiritual practice: for years I viewed spiritual paths sym-pathetically, read with interest and applauded from the side-lines—yet remained a spectator, unchanged by my intellectual explorations. Even now I resist the plunge into actual practice, surrender, and transformation.

Friends frequently use the word "practice" (as in "faith and practice"), but I had thought of Quaker practice as simply how Quakers behave when they live by Quaker values. Missing from my simplistic understanding was recognition of the strenuous effort, commitment, and risk required to live truly in the Light. Missing also was the notion of practice as practicing: trying and failing, trying again and again—repeated efforts over a lifetime to bring order into the chaos of my life. Christian writers speak of this sustained effort as the imitation of Christ. Although mo-nastic traditions hold up the ideal of a wholly God-inspired life, lay religious practice (and, if truth be told, most monastic prac-tice as well) typically drifts far from such an ideal.

Early Friends expressly rejected world-renouncing monasti-cism; but they did not endorse in its place an easy, undemand-ing spirituality; rather, they cautioned against succumbing to the seductive charms of a "worldly" life. They knew the devastation and fierce joy of seeking to do God's will in one's life and in the world, as one empties of self and grows into what one most truly is.

Books of Quaker *Faith and Practice* are traditionally called *Book of Discipline*, another word I had passed over too readily. In an age of instant gratification and comfort, "discipline" often rings of punishment for wrongdoing, with no resonance of the straitening pleasures of self-transcendence through submission to an exacting regimen. Significant accomplishment in most walks of life requires a paradoxical combination of strenuous application and surrender of self-will. I found it easy to recognize a demanding path to excellence in challenging educational endeavors, high-level athletic performance, skilled artistic expression, and elsewhere, even when I chose not to walk on it. But in spiritual matters I favored an easier, more comfortable route, sitting down each week in meeting for worship and hoping that without any risk or commitment, lightning would strike.

With its physically challenging postures, its long periods of carefully composed immobility and its cultural tradition of austerity, Zen gives the lie to such spiritual laziness. But I would not have needed to engage in Buddhist meditation to realize this fact, had I faced squarely the demands of my original faith. To confirm this claim, one does not have to seek far; in order to map out a lifetime of challenging spiritual growth, Friends need only to pick up a copy of *Faith and Practice* from their own yearly meeting, read carefully its counsel on spiritual formation (including its advices and queries), and then open themselves in vulnerability to the searching Light that calls for faithfulness to these many guidelines. This is a task that no one will fully complete.

Without appropriate guidance in such efforts, we may not deepen insight, but our sense of failure. As a boy in a Quaker family, I learned many lessons about what I should and should not do in meeting for worship. These expectations mainly concerned my outward behavior, however—not my inner process. Though sometimes moved by the power and presence of my fellow worshippers, I had no clue as to how to find my own way to such depths. Hunger for spiritual awakening coupled with my inability to find it in meeting for worship ultimately drove me to Zen. There, I found a wealth of direction about the uses of silence. With help from more experienced teachers, I came upon an inward healing path. Because this journey led me not away from myself but more deeply into my own nature, I began to recover childhood visions—hints of wholeness and joy from springs that had seemed dry. I had been viewing Quaker spirituality through a veil accumulated over centuries, an unnoticed conceptual overlay that had distanced me from the living Spirit. Vibrant, unsettling Truth had become prosaic and quaint, leaving me unmoved. I had shrunk from direct experience of Divine power.

A Quaker Spiritual Practice

In the quest to know God, some yearn for quiet inwardness and repose, others are drawn to ecstatic devotional practices, and yet others find their religious impulses most freely expressed in an active life of engagement, of working in the world. In the white-hot crucible of the early Friends' movement, these various strands were virtually fused, often in the same person—inner surrender to the Light was expressed in charismatic, bodily outbursts of religious passion and in courageous strength for public witness and activism. This spiritual power arose not from a new set of doctrines and beliefs, but from Friends' discovery of an experiential path to direct encounter with God. The ministry of George Fox is rife with instruction on this path. Though he repeatedly corrected what he saw as false interpretations of the Christian message, Fox sought above all to direct others to their own inward teacher, the Christ within. No contemporary scholar of early Quakerism has seen this point more clearly than English Friend Rex Ambler.[9] In a groundbreaking anthology of extracts from the writings of Fox, *Truth of the Heart*, Ambler writes,

> Fox had a distinctive approach of his own, which was not consciously drawing on any of the traditions he inherited. He was not, for example, presenting a teaching that people were expected to believe and follow... . He was telling them rather to do something, because what they needed to make them free and fulfilled as human beings, "perfect", was in them, and it was in them already without their having to imbibe it from a church or teaching outside.

It was an inner awareness which would enable them initially "to see themselves" as they were, in reality, beyond the deceptions of "the self", but then also to see what they and others could become, and should become... . (I)t in effect challenged everyone to find their own inner truth, and to learn to trust it and live by it... . There was, in fact, for both individual and group, a distinct process to be undergone.[10]

Ambler's assertion that "there was... a distinct process to be undergone" confirms the judgment of Douglas Gwyn: "there was some degree of technique to early Quaker spirituality..., guidance that helped refocus spiritual energies from ego-centered striving to true surrender."[11]

Gwyn refers to a spiritual "technique"; Ambler writes of "a distinct process to be undergone." What was this technique, this process? What did Fox ask his listeners to do? The most suggestive answers to this question that I have found are in Fox's writings from the first years of the burgeoning Quaker movement. In restating his spiritual guidance in contemporary language, I find myself returning to familiar terms of Quaker worship, now viewed in a radically revealing light.

Being Still

Stand still in that which is pure, after you see yourselves, and then mercy comes in. After you see your thoughts and the temptations, do not think but submit. Then the Power comes. Stand still in the Light and submit to it, and the other will be hushed and gone. Then contentment comes. When temptations and troubles appear, sink down in that which is pure, and all will be hushed and fly away. Your strength is to stand still.

—George Fox[12]

The practice of "waiting upon the Lord" in silence is a discipline that halts our nervous compulsions and forces us to "stew in our own juices," uncomfortable as that may be. In speaking of the true worship of God, George Fox often quoted God's gentle rebuke to Peter to stop and listen to Christ. "Be still and know that I am God" is the way the Psalmist articulated it. (Psalm 46:10)

—Douglas Gwyn[13]

Sitting in deep stillness, opening to the moment, suspending all my efforts to be "more than God hath made," I recognize that my many visceral impulses—to shift, fidget, look about, scratch, or make other bodily adjustments—all arise from underlying unease with my condition. Like others, I have cultivated a wide range of largely unconscious strategies for avoiding uncomfortable sensations, thoughts, and feelings, so that I might look elsewhere instead of into myself. The discipline of stillness is painful and humbling but also cleansing, as I open to layers of experience from which I had averted my gaze.

Despite many years of experience in Friends' meetings for worship, I first practiced such deep stillness in Zen meditation retreats. Only later did I find it affirmed within Quakerism itself. The quotation from Fox above is explicit: "Your strength is to stand still." Before meeting houses were constructed to house their gatherings, Friends sometimes quite literally obeyed Fox's injunction to "Stand still in the light." Douglas Gwyn reports that "It frightened neighbors to see as many as two or three hundred men, women, and children standing in silence out in a field, in meetings that might go on for hours."[14]

In a brief piece from the pages of *Friends Journal*, contemporary English Friend Caroline Jones emphasizes the importance of physical stillness:

To sink down to the seed we need not only silence, we need also stillness. When we adults fidget in Quaker meeting, we unconsciously reinforce our habitual ways of thinking and being and doing. Fidgeting is a way of avoiding something. When we sit still we come closer to who we are and are more able to observe the shifting sands of the mind that we label I, me, and mine ... . Stillness is disturbing. No wonder we fidget and look around and cough; we want to hide from ourselves, from each other, and from God ... . Physical stillness is a training ground where we can learn to be less neurotic and more wise. When we practice stillness together in worship, it helps us to become one body, a larger conduit for love and healing.

Physical stillness promotes mental calm. By remaining still and not obeying every impulse to adjust the body, thoughts quiet down and it is easier to discern which ones to act on. By allowing the body to be still, we notice the subtler, more essential movements of life: the breath, the blood, sounds from inside and outside, the movement of air across the skin. When our bodies are relaxed and alert, we see beyond our usual preoccupations and are more available to new insight ... . Fidgeting keeps us on the surface; stillness takes us into the depths where we learn to "be no more than God hath made."[15]

Being Present

Give not way to the lazy, dreaming mind.

—George Fox[16]

Even today ... few people can sit through an hour of silent Quaker worship without a wandering mind which dodges painfully away from steady reflection. The first efforts at stillness begin to show a person his inadequacy, emptiness of purpose, or well-buried guilt.

—Hugh Barbour[17]

Silent Friends' worship may seem to be a time for uplifting reverie, an opportunity to cultivate inspirational thoughts and pleasantly soothing reflections. Quaker worship then appears under the guise of a subdued escape into an attractive fantasy world. However pleasant (and however widespread) such a use of the silence may be, it is surely not what Fox and other early Quakers intended, not what "waiting upon the Lord" is about. Their writings emphasize not only physical stillness, but even more, a stillness of thought and will. Isaac Penington's words provide a brisk clinic for clarity: "Give over thine own willing; give over thine own running; give over thine own desiring to know or to be any thing, and sink down to the seed... ." I must drop the strivings of my small self if I am to surrender to the presence of Christ within.

Those who have attempted to still their minds for more than a moment will have discovered how difficult it is to do so. Some Asian traditions speak of "monkey mind," jumping uncontrollably from here to there to elsewhere without any repose or tranquility. Zen teaching compares an untrained mind to a wild ox that requires many years of taming. Referring to "temptations and troubles," George Fox puts his finger upon the two primary sources of this agitation of the mind—desire and fear. Craving this, fleeing that, I lose myself in elaborate mental fantasies. I obsess about the past and future, rehearsing this or that scenario. In contrast, the discipline of stillness requires that I "do not think but submit." Eminent Quaker scholar John Punshon writes, "The stillness of a Friends' meeting is a state of great attentiveness, not of abandon."[18] Rather than drifting with "the lazy, dreaming mind," committed silent worship calls me back from my fantasies to the immediacy of the present moment, to "stand still in the Light and submit to it."

Knowing Myself

The central spiritual insight that inspired 17th-century Quakerism was that Christ has come to teach his people himself,[19] that "The God who spoke still speaks."[20] And if God is speaking to me, should not I be listening? Many ruefully report that when they listen inwardly, all that they hear is themselves—fantasies and fears, arguments and rehearsals, distractions and preoccupations. Fox saw that such listening is not a failure of worship, however, but a necessary first step in worship itself. In order to hear beneath the chatter of my mind, I must first awaken to the chatter itself. "See your thoughts and temptations," says Fox. Expanding upon his advice, the weighty 18th-century Friend Samuel Bownas declared that "It is ... highly needful for us to learn *to know* ourselves, and to keep in it daily, and not to forget and lose the sense of the imperfections and defects in the natural constitution of our own minds."[21]

As my own experience makes all too clear, a true encounter with oneself can be far from comforting. Leading Quaker scholar Hugh Barbour observes of early Friends, "The light that ultimately gave joy, peace, and guidance gave at first only terror."[22] Yet to see our thoughts and temptations, to know ourselves, is not to wallow blindly in our troubles while we await a magical rescue from above. Fox tells us to "take heed of being hurried with many thoughts but live in that which goes over them."[23] After I see myself, I should "stand still in that which is pure" and "be stayed in the principle of God." What do these directions mean—and how am I to follow them?

When I struggle with my obsessions, it may seem that I have only two options—to become caught up in my distress, or to push it aside and force my mind to dwell on other things. Fox points to another way, one in which I attend to my inner turmoil without descending into it:

What the light doth make manifest and discover, temptations, confusions, distractions, ... do not look at (them) but at the light that ... makes them manifest ... . For looking down at sin, and corruption, and distraction, you are swallowed up in it; but looking at the light that discovers them, you will see over them. That will give victory; and you will find grace and strength; and there is the first step of peace.[24]

Seeing my thoughts, cravings, and fears without being drawn into them, I move from self-preoccupation to awareness of a larger reality. This liberating viewpoint is the Light—not a glowing object in my mind's eye, but rather that which enables me to see my troubles while freeing me from immersion in them. Standing still in the Light, I yield to expansive openness and presence; in the words of Penington and Fox, I find "sweet experience" and "contentment." As early Friend Elizabeth Hendricks writes, I aim to "keep close to the Light, and feel the Power of God, and abide in it, and let it be (my) daily care, to remain in the Awe and Fear of God continually... ."[25] Perhaps no phrase is more characteristic of the ministry of George Fox than his simple words, "Live in the Life of God, and feel it."[26]

The Moment of Truth

Walk in the Truth... stand all naked, bare and uncovered before the Lord.

—George Fox[27]

Because this process is uncomfortable—I am, after all, experiencing the very parts of myself that I seek to ignore—patience and courage are required. Worship is a form of cleansing, as I lay myself open to God without reservation. John Punshon puts the point uncompromisingly: "I must be willing to open my heart completely, give everything I have and hold nothing back in my own secret places. I must, in a word, be willing to be searched myself."[28] Margaret Fell counsels fellow Quakers: "Now, Friends... let the Eternal Light search you... for this will deal plainly with you, it will rip you up, and lay you open... naked and bare before the Lord God, from whom you cannot hide yourselves."[29] As noted by Howard Brinton, Friends' silent worship has much in common with a spiritual practice made famous by a simple Catholic monk, Brother Lawrence, "the practice of the presence of God."[30] When I feel that every action I perform, every thought I entertain, is seen through and through by a Divine eye, I have no recourse but to let go and to surrender fully.

Vulnerability to God is also vulnerability to each other. The gathered worship of a true Friends meeting is not merely a cover of silence under which individuals quietly "do their own thing"; it is a shared endeavor in which many wills simultaneously yield up their separateness so that all may "come to know the hidden unity in the Eternal Being."[31] In such an act of corporate submission, the meeting opens to the power of Truth.

Early Friends' concept of Truth was thus no mere correspondence of a statement with a state of affairs, nor a bold reporting of the facts, but rather an alignment of the whole being with an electrifying Reality, a riveting, enveloping Presence. Describing George Fox as he rose in meeting to pray, William Penn hints at this power: "The most awful, living, reverent frame I ever felt or beheld, I must say, was his in prayer. And truly... he knew and lived nearer to the Lord than other men... ."[32] Such an alignment may signal itself by dramatic shuddering of the body, or more gently by a wordless sweetness stealing over all who are present, as described by Francis Howgill: "As we waited upon him in pure silence, our minds out of all things, his heavenly presence appeared in our assemblies, when there was no language, tongue, nor speech from any creature."[33] If we wonder about the rapid growth of Quakerism in 17th-century England, we need look no further than to such infusions of Spirit, when "the Power of the Lord is over all."

The moment of Truth is also a moment of *conviction*: not mere persuasion, but (as in a court of law) being thoroughly seen for who one is. Abandoning private agendas, giving up and yielding, being "crucified"—humbled and transformed by the Light so that an old self dies and a new one is born—this radical rebirth is as rare as it is precious.

The Challenge of Integrity

All ye that profess, see that you possess, and profess no more than you are.

—George Fox[34]

For anyone honest and courageous enough to "stand still in the Light" and allow it to "rip you up and lay you open... naked and bare before the Lord God," life can never be the same. Pretense becomes impossible; posturing is a distasteful charade. Surrendering to Truth means that I must live the insight that I have gained. This transformation does not happen overnight; it is the ongoing work of a lifetime. But in the light of Truth, nothing else suffices but to become what I know.

George Fox was thoroughly familiar with those who professed Christian faith and doctrine, but who did not live it from its Source, who had not "walked in the light." He called such hypocrites "professors" (a delicious irony to this emeritus professor), holding them in low esteem. Quakers are not immune from such subtle hypocrisy, to be sure. William Penn cautions his fellow Friends against their own version of spiritual bad faith in meeting for worship:

> When you come to your meetings... what do you do? Do you then gather together bodily only, and kindle a fire, compassing yourselves about with the sparks of your own kindling, and so please yourselves, and walk in the "Light of your own fire, and in the sparks which you have kindled"...? Or rather, do you sit down in True Silence, resting from your own Will and Workings, and waiting upon the Lord, with your minds fixed in that Light wherewith Christ has enlightened you, until the Lord breathes life in you, refresheth you, and prepares you, and your spirits and souls, to make you fit for his service, that you may offer unto him a pure and spiritual sacrifice?[35]

As Penn's questions make clear, Quaker integrity goes beyond mere consistency. To live in accord with one's professed values is to avoid an obvious form of hypocrisy, to be sure; but until one has surrendered oneself to the workings of the Spirit and has become "a Child of Light, and hast walked in the light," that consistency is merely formal, lacking the authentic spontaneity of a truly faithful life.

Quaker integrity also implies restraint. Fox observed an absence of self-control in the Ranters, a sometimes Spirit-inspired but often undisciplined religious movement that was contemporaneous with early Quakerism and frequently conflated with it. Fox said of the Ranters that "they did not wait upon God... to gather their minds together to feel his presence and power and therein to sit to wait upon him, for they had spoken themselves dry and had spent their portions and not lived in that which they spake."[36] Caught up in the enthusiasm of new insight, I may profess more than I possess. To yield to this temptation is to outrun my leading; instead I should stay low, remaining within my portion of the Light, taking care to profess no more than I am.

A God at Hand

Surely, this commandment that I am commanding you today is not too hard for you, nor is it too far away. It is not in heaven, that you should say, "Who will go up to heaven for us, and get it for us so that we may hear it and observe it?" Neither is it beyond the sea, that you should say, "Who will cross to the other side of the sea for us, and get it for us so that we may hear it and observe it?" No, the word is very near to you; it is in your mouth and in your heart for you to observe.

—Deuteronomy 30:11-14

When I am no more than God hath made, I open to the truth of my life. No longer straining to be elsewhere, I feel less

43

urgency, more clarity, and comfort. The penumbra of distracting anxiety surrounding my mind, sapping my energy and purpose, is acknowledged and eased by inward opening to the Light.

My experience widens and deepens—and wonder creeps in at the margins. Like a fish that for the first time becomes aware of the ocean in which it swims, I awaken to unbounded intimacy, a benign and encompassing love, a searching light over all, a sense of bathing in and being permeated by blessedness. Momentarily I no longer exist; there is only the experience of being known. Realizing that all is well, I smile. Nothing can eradicate such blessedness. My usual complaints are inconsequential. Generous insights come unbidden. I have no doubt that this aura of beatitude is the love of God, the blessed release, the "peace of God, which surpasses all understanding." (Philippians 4:7)

Such moments fade, and I once again shrink into my small self. But my memory lingers, lending conviction to my faith, offering reassurance even in distress. More at ease with my unease, I see over that which would draw me down, and am less captive to its constraints. As I am freed for constructive engagement with the world, I give myself to the work before me.

The treasures that I have found in my Quaker hearth demand earnest polishing and sustained care. I must guard against leaving them once again in the ashes, forgotten. In private moments of the day and in corporate worship with others, turning inward to be still in the Light, I learn, moment by moment, to live in the Life of God, and feel it.

CHAPTER THREE

PURE PASSION

Until we bow down and bear the suffering of life—not opposing it, but absorbing it and being it—we cannot see what our life is. This by no means implies passivity or non-action, but action from a state of complete acceptance. Even "acceptance" is not quite accurate—it's simply being the suffering. It isn't a matter of protecting ourselves, or accepting something else. Complete openness, complete vulnerability to life is (surprisingly enough) the only satisfactory way of living our life.

—Charlotte Joko Beck[1]

We must weep before we can laugh.

—Lin Yutang[2]

On Waxen Wings

Gathering myself in August 1957 for my first year of college, I sip a heady brew of fear, eagerness, and over-weening ambition. This intoxication is briefly sobered by a disconcerting tone, however: a poem composed for

45

me by our quiet Quaker neighbor, Edith Smith. Edith has known me since infancy and has followed my growth to the cusp of manhood with reticent, kindly eyes. No mere doggerel wishing me bon voyage, Edith's poem voices her misgivings about my way forward. Soon I have lost the copy that she had given to me. I now recall only the first four lines:

> *Like proud and headlong Icarus, into the path*
> *Of the rising sun, he is gone without goodbyes.*
> *For him, the eager, lurks no aftermath*
> *Behind the hope in his far-fixed eyes.*

At the time I am only dimly aware of the ancient myth of Icarus, who flew on waxen wings too close to the sun, then crashed into the sea. I regard Edith with condescension, as a timid, inhibited soul who is so concerned with propriety that she has never truly lived. I thank her for her efforts and silently dismiss her concern.

Yet Edith was wiser than I knew. My waxen wings carried me ever higher for 17 years, then melted in the heat of apparent success—and I plunged into depression and despair. For many years thereafter I was emotionally and spiritually at sea, struggling to stay afloat while assembling my own life raft.

Icarus did not see himself clearly, nor did I. What were the roots of this blindness? Though I cannot speak for Icarus, I now see more clearly the contours of my own youthful confusion. Fearing that I was profoundly flawed, I compensated by compulsive pursuit of external success. I saw the hollowness of these efforts only years later, when I slid into a losing endgame of alcohol and substance abuse. In the words of AA, I "hit bottom."

Before I can hope for transformation, I must see myself clearly. My first painful efforts come through psychotherapy, a challenging exercise in self-honesty. Slowly I unravel the tangled web of my life and expose it to the light. Feeling a need to "come clean," in my first summer of sobriety, I write a confession of my misbehaviors and give it to my wife, who has borne the heaviest burden. (I learn later that this exercise is similar to Step Four of AA, which requires "a searching and fearless moral inventory of ourselves.")[3]

As I drop my resistance to truth, I awaken to a new world. My vision clears, my awareness deepens—and I am given the gift of aligning my life with reality. Blessed by small moments of grace, I discern my next steps and find strength to take them.

The Paradoxical Theory of Change

Know thyself.
—The Oracle at Delphi

If you want to know God, learn to know yourself first.
—Evagrius Ponticus[4]

Resolving to introduce my nascent insights into my professional life, in spring 1975 I taught a new philosophy class to help students to clarify for themselves their vision of the life they hoped to live.[5] Because I had benefitted from my own efforts at honest self-assessment, I began the course with a paper assignment, "A Look At Myself," in which I asked students to describe their present state and declare their personal goals for their participation in the course.[6] Before the paper was due, I shared with them some of my own struggles, hoping that my candor would be infectious. Over decades of tracking their development, I observed that students who took the risk to describe themselves honestly were also the ones who later reported the most significant insight and growth. In contrast, those who played it safe (claiming that they already knew everything that they needed to know) used the course to confirm their prejudices and to rationalize standing pat.

I observed this pattern also in group psychotherapy. Breakthroughs of healing and growth occurred when we surrendered to the moment and acknowledged the hard truths of our lives. In contrast, steadfast denial assured only that we remained stuck. I came upon a study of the therapeutic technique of Fritz Perls, the noted Gestalt therapist, that gave theoretical underpinning to these observations. Perls did not advise his patients; rather, he simply described with devastating candor what he saw in their lives. If they accepted the truth of his observations, their self-awareness deepened and their lives rounded into greater wholeness. Describing his approach, Perls said simply that awareness in itself is healing. In a widely cited paper, Arnold Beisser defined the core assumption of Perls' psychotherapeutic technique as "the paradoxical theory of change": *Change occurs when I become what I am, not when I try to become what I am not.*[7]

This concise piece of analysis helped me to recognize the secret of what I had seen in Alcoholics Anonymous, in psychotherapy, and among my students: if we refuse to see and acknowledge who we are, and instead struggle to mold ourselves into preconceived images of health and success, we only bury our unresolved issues more deeply and become less authentic. On the other hand, when we fully accept the reality of our present state, we are freed—and our lives unfold in healing growth.

In Zen practice I found a rigorous application of the paradoxical theory of change, as well as elegant concepts to express it. Compulsions of the mind arise from attachment (*tanha*, or thirst, in Sanskrit)—aversion and craving that give rise to fantasies of safety and satisfaction. Through systematic training in *zazen*, the meditative practice of Zen, we practice the art of suspending this passive drift. Rather than retreating constantly into thoughts of the future or the past, we develop courage to live in the present moment. Through disciplined attention, we remain in place and experience our impulse to escape—coming face to face with our underlying distress.

The discomfort of this discipline is most pronounced during extended meditation retreats (called *sesshin*) in which one sits for lengthy periods in a carefully-prescribed posture, maintaining silence and stillness, returning again and again to one's breath, facing one's demons as they arise—not to exorcise them, but simply to be present to them. Unresolved childhood traumas bubble up; the pain of a broken relationship hits with full force; self-deception becomes obvious; false hopes die. The teachings counsel us to drop all resistance, all efforts to avoid the truth, and surrender to the reality of our lives. Out of this descent into our own private purgatory gradually unfolds a life of wholeness and equanimity. In August 1995 during a five-day *sesshin* at the Zen Center of San Diego, one such hellish yet healing moment came upon me:

> *Sitting on my zafu facing the wall, I relive a buried childhood trauma: while drinking at a water fountain, I am suddenly kicked in the seat of the pants by a girl whom I know from school. As she walks away, I stand dumbfounded, gripped by shame and utter impotence—nothing but a piece of shit. Reliving my memory, I become consumed by intense, unadulterated hatred, which appears in my mind's eye as a pulsing, brownish-red ball. Gradually my anguish subsides. In the aftermath comes a wave of relief, and I find that my buried hostility has eased.*

This incident is an object lesson in *zazen*, which requires that *I pay full attention to this moment*—to the immediacy of my sensory experience. Noting my thoughts yet not yielding to another round of obsessive rumination, I return to direct awareness of my body. I do not attempt to change my experience; I do not suppress or try to overcome it. Instead I pay close attention, observing my compulsion to go somewhere else. Finally the root of my resistance reveals itself as buried pain or fear. Knotted pain unravels. In this wordless awareness of my suffering, I am cleansed. I become at home within my skin, more at peace, and more alive to the joy of living.

One of the most beloved Western teachers of Buddhism, Pema Chodron, gives this counsel:

> Pause, take three conscious breaths, and lean in. Lean into the energy. Abide with it. Experience it fully. Taste it. Touch it. Smell it. Get curious about it. How does it feel in your body? What thoughts does it give birth to?... Just do not speak, do not act, and feel the energy. Be one with your own energy, one with the ebb and flow of life. Rather than rejecting the energy, embrace it. This leaning in is very open, very curious and intelligent.... Then relax and move on.[8]

As we become less self-obsessed, our natural compassion emerges. Anxiety eases—and small joys break into awareness. We are more adaptable and creative. A traditional Buddhist image for this transformation is the lotus flower, "at home in the muddy water."

There are, to be sure, varieties of meditation that seek to transport us elsewhere—forms of "spiritual materialism"[9] that promise escape from "the muddy water." In my experience, those who give themselves to such practices fall into one of two groups: the few who have achieved an overwhelming "enlightenment experience" and see themselves as members of a spiritual elite (while secretly retaining their character flaws)—and the many who yearn for such experiences, viewing their present life with distaste.

During the early years of my Zen practice, I was consumed by just such yearnings. Joko treated my spiritual fantasies kindly, since they are common among beginners. Yet she consistently redirected my attention to the very present that I was trying to avoid—the actual texture of my experience, moment to moment. Joko devised a practice chant (used daily at the Zen Center of San Diego) to summarize this core teaching:

Caught in a self-centered dream—only suffering.
Holding to self-centered thoughts—exactly the dream.
Each moment, life as it is, the only teacher;
Being just this moment, compassion's way.

One of Joko's senior students, Barry Magid, writes that "the fundamental paradox of (meditative) practice is that leaving everything alone is itself what is ultimately transformative."[10] This is a transparent restatement of the paradoxical theory of change.

Jon Kabat-Zinn, a major contributor to the movement of mindfulness meditation from the fringes into the mainstream of contemporary Western culture (including medical and psycho-therapeutic practice), summarizes the point in admirably lucid language:

Meditation is not about trying to get anywhere else. It is about allowing yourself to be exactly where you are and as you are, and for the world to be exactly as it is in this moment as well... . the paradox is that you can only change yourself or the world if you get out of your own way for a moment, and give yourself over and trust in allow-ing things to be as they already are, without pursuing any-thing, especially goals that are products of your thinking. Einstein put it quite cogently: "The problems that exist in the world today cannot be solved by the level of thinking that created them." ... We need to return to our original, untouched, unconditioned mind. How can we do this? Pre-cisely by taking a moment... to get outside of the stream of thought and sit by the bank and rest for a while in things as they are underneath our thinking... . That means being with what is for a moment, and trusting what is deepest and best in yourself, even if it doesn't make any sense to the thinking mind.[11]

When we open without reservation to the present moment, we awaken to hidden resources within ourselves, unexpected gifts of grace—creativity, compassionate energy, new perspectives, fresh insights. Kabat-Zinn writes, "dropping in on the bare experience of the present moment is actually dropping in on just the qualities you may be hoping to cultivate—because they all come out of awareness, and it is awareness that we fall into when we stop trying to get somewhere or to have a special feeling... . Awareness itself is the teacher, the student, and the lesson."[12]

Kabat-Zinn's disclosure of the heart of meditation dispels the misconception that meditative practice is a retreat into a passive inner citadel, insulating oneself from the suffering and injustice of the world. Passivity is acquiescence to the status quo, stepping back from our own raw energy and natural vitality. In contrast, mindfulness opens us to these very realities. Instead of shrinking from our experience, we yield to it; rather than remaining imprisoned by fear, we take the risk to become all that we are in this moment. Awareness floats lightly upon the waves of experience, like a lotus upon rippling water. We do not rein in our positive energy, but express it in spontaneous activity. Yielding to the fullness of the moment, we become more sensitive to the needs of those around us. Work becomes playful and joyous, releasing energies that we did not know we possessed.

Just such an explosion of exuberant and healing energy is seen in the extraordinary growth of 17th-century Friends. The fruit of standing still in the Light, "all naked, bare and uncovered before the Lord,"[13] is to become *real* in this present moment. A veil drops away, and one awakens to the grace and the joy of a new creation. Fox's challenging counsel to set aside all agendas and surrender fully to the truth of our present condition is yet another iteration of the paradoxical theory of change.

From Self-Centeredness to Reality-Centeredness

To be self-centered is to be off center from life itself.
—Marc Ian Barasch[14]

John Hick, the eminent English philosopher of religion, declared, "The function of religion, as (our) response to ultimate Reality, is to transform human existence from self-centeredness to Reality-centeredness."[15] Setting aside our narcissistic self-preoccupation, suspending striving, we open to the intimacy of the present moment and align ourselves with its truth. This pattern is found not only in Hinduism, Taoism, and Buddhism, but also in the three great Western traditions. In his classic study, *The Varieties of Religious Experience*, William James describes this shift:

> The transition from tenseness, self-responsibility, and worry to equanimity, receptivity, and peace, is the most wonderful of all those shiftings of inner equilibrium, those changes of the personal center of energy, which I have analyzed so often; and the chief wonder of it is that it so often comes about, not by doing, but by simply relaxing and throwing the burden down. This abandonment of self-responsibility seems to be the fundamental act in specifically religious, as distinct from moral practice."[16]

One of the many paradoxes of spiritual practice is that the generality of abstraction locks us into a prison of our own making, whereas when we open to the immediacy of this particular moment, we awaken to our unity with the world. In familiar words, William Blake invites us:

> To see a world in a grain of sand
> And heaven in a wildflower,
> Hold infinity in the palm of your hand
> And eternity in an hour.[17]

A similar sentiment is captured succinctly in a few lines by the medieval Japanese Zen master, Dogen Zenji: "To study the self is to forget the self; to forget the self is to awaken to the ten thousand things." Ruben Habito, a Jesuit priest who is "the first Catholic whose experience of enlightenment was authenticated by recognized Zen masters," cites the Japanese term *botsunyu* ("to lose oneself and enter") to convey this intimate surrender. Habito writes, "Zen enlightenment involves a stance of readiness to plunge right into the very heart of the world, in solidarity with all the joys and hopes, the pains and sufferings, the blood, sweat, and tears of all sentient beings—right here and now."[18]

During a session at the Zen Center of San Diego in November 1984 I gain a small taste of such wonder:

On Sunday morning while waiting to see Joko, I experience a mini-opening: an unannounced aura of beatitude, of appreciation, in which the ordinariness of things about me seems invested with magical presence, a distinct flavor of wonder, of "suchness"; this moment blossoms into a small epiphany.

Metanoia

Every seeker of Ultimate Mystery has to pass through interior death and rebirth, perhaps many times over.
—Father Thomas Keating[19]

Salvation comes only when we can say, "Father, into thy hands I entrust my spirit," or "Lord, though thou slay me, yet will I trust in thee." This is resignation or self-surrender... ready to have "thy will" prevail upon a world of finite beings. This is the characteristic attitude of a religious mind toward life and the world.
—D.T. Suzuki[20]

Many years into my recovery, I came across a concept that names my experience of death and rebirth: *metanoia*. From the

Greek, the term "denotes a change of mind, a reorientation, a fundamental transformation of outlook, of an individual's vision of the world and of him/herself, and a new way of loving others and the Universe." Though commonly associated in Christian theology with repentance of sin, the scope of metanoia goes beyond dwelling upon one's failures and shortcomings, to a lifting of past burdens and an awakening to "natural glory and freedom." In Carl Jung's psychological theory, metanoia names the disintegration of rigid, limiting patterns of psychological functioning, making way for emotional rebirth and regeneration.[21] AMA Samy, a contemporary Zen teacher, relates the following Christian account of metanoia, so rich that I quote him at length:

> Let me give you the radical conversion story of the Polish-American Jesuit priest, Walter Ciszek. ...During the Soviet occupation of Poland during World War II, Walter entered Russia disguised as a worker but was soon discovered and taken prisoner by the NKVD and... asked to admit and sign that he was a spy. ... He felt he was the defender of his country, his Church and his God and was determined that he would never betray them. But finally, with the incessant questioning and threats he broke down.... In his own words: "Then one day the blackness closed in around me completely... . I had reached a point of despair. I was overwhelmed by the hopelessness of my situation... . I knew that I had gone beyond all bounds, had crossed over the brink into a fit of blackness I had never known before. It was very real and I began to tremble. I was scared and ashamed, the victim of a new sense of guilt and humiliation... . For that one moment of blackness, I had lost not only hope but the last shreds of my faith in God. I had stood alone in a void and I had not even thought of or recalled the one thing that had been my constant guide, my only source of consolation in all other failures, my ultimate recourse: I had lost the sight of God."

Then Walter remembered Jesus in the Garden of Gethsemane praying to God, "Not as I will, but as thou wilt."
Jesus' prayer was not just conformity to the will of God;
it was total self-surrender, a stripping away of all human
fears, of all doubts about his own abilities to withstand the
Passion, of every last shred of self including self-doubt... .
"I can only call it a conversion experience, and I can only
tell you frankly that my life was changed from that moment
on. If my moment of despair had been a moment of total
blackness, then this was an experience of blinding light.
... Up until now, I had always seen my role... in the divine
economy as an active one. Up to this time, I had retained
in my own hands the reins of all decisions, actions, and endeavor; I saw it as my task to 'co-operate' with his grace,
to be involved to the end in the working out of salvation.
God's will was 'out there' somewhere, hidden, yet clear and
unmistakable. It was my role... to discover what it was and
then conform my will to that, and so work at achieving the
ends of his divine providence. I remained...the master of
my own destiny. Perfection consisted simply in learning to
discover God's will in every situation and then in bending
every effort to do what must be done. Now, with sudden
and almost blinding clarity and simplicity, I realized I had
been trying to do something with my own will and intellect
that was at once too much and mostly all wrong. God's will
was not hidden somewhere 'out there' in the situations in
which I found myself; the situations themselves were his
will for me. What he wanted was for me to accept these situations as from his hands, to let go of the reins and place
myself entirely at his disposal. He was asking of me an act
of total trust, allowing for no exceptions, no areas where I
could set conditions or seem to hesitate. He was asking a
complete gift of self, nothing held back."[22]

AMA Samy reports that as Walter makes this "complete gift of
self," he is flooded with "blinding light," swept up in "a fresh new

wave of confidence and happiness..., born to a new world and new self.... . He has let go trying to control all of life and reality and learnt to surrender himself to mystery that is graciousness. His heart has found its abiding place in... equanimity... . It is his 'yes' to the Mystery that is emptiness, and at the same time it is the great 'yes' of Reality to his being and existence."[23]

The Cross Event

The language of Walter Ciszek's spiritual transformation recalls St. Paul's challenge: "I appeal to you therefore, brothers and sisters... to present your bodies as a living sacrifice, holy and acceptable to God, which is your spiritual worship." (Romans 12:1) This image is inspired by the archetypal metaphor of Christianity, the "cross event"—the Passion of Christ. No portion of Christian scripture has been more thoroughly analyzed or variously interpreted. My purpose here is modest, to offer my own personal responses to the story.

Current use of the word "passion" obscures the earliest meaning of this term. We think of passion as unleashed emotion: yielding to impulse, an uncontrolled flood of fear or desire. Yet in dictionary entries for "passion," the usual first meaning is "the suffering of pain"—where "to suffer" means "to allow" or "to receive."[24] (In Medieval Latin, the term that is translated as "passion," *passio*, is contrasted to "action.") The Passion of Christ begins with the story of the Garden of Gethsemane, where we see Jesus wrestling with the choice before him, pleading with God ("Abba") to be relieved of his burden. The turning point—the metanoia—of the Passion is the moment when Jesus surrenders his own human wishes and says in utter sincerity, "Not my will but yours be done."

Christians have expressed this insight in various ways: there can be no "cheap grace"; no peace of heart without "taking up one's cross"; no "victorious Christian living" without "suffering unto death." Quaker scholar Michael Birkel describes the views of early Friends: pure motivation arises from holy surrender, "resignation," "dying and rising with Christ."[25] When we become willing to face our lives honestly, our vision is clarified and our hearts are freed.

The spiritual regeneration of Walter Ciszek follows the pattern that we find in the Passion of Christ. Ciszek now understands that "God's will was not hidden somewhere 'out there' in the situations in which I found myself; the situations themselves were his will for me. What he wanted was for me to accept these situations as from his hands, to let go of the reins and place myself entirely at his disposal." Likewise, Jesus does not deliberate between competing legalistic obligations; rather, he struggles inwardly, then accepts that his present dire situation is God's will for him—and makes "a complete gift of self." The remainder of the Passion story plays out the inevitable consequences of this decision. Even as the agony of the crucifixion awakens our sympathy, our interpretation of it as a supreme act of loving sacrifice on behalf of creation grounds a deeper reverence and devotion.

It will be apparent to those who are familiar with the main strands of Christian theology that I do not endorse the traditional doctrine of "substitution" according to which Jesus' death was a singular historical event that once and for all lifted the burden of sin and suffering from humanity, freeing us to enjoy a promise of salvation that had formerly been unavailable; rather, I believe that this promise has always, in all places, been implicit in the human condition.

The Idolatry of Orthodoxy

The true light… enlightens everyone.
—John 1:9

Even less do I believe that literal acceptance of the sacrificial act of the historical Jesus is essential for spiritual redemption.

Rather, I see the story of the Passion as the reflection of a universal archetype: regardless of our cultural and religious backgrounds, each of us daily chooses either to avoid the reality of our lives or to face ourselves honestly and open to the wisdom that lies within.

As a boy I heard my father reading reverentially from the King James Version of the Bible. My spiritual life took form around its language, and the Bible remains my primary religious "comfort food." Yet I recognize that persons raised in other religious traditions find their own spiritual nourishment in the language and rituals of those traditions. In keeping with my Quaker tradition, I believe that the elements of an authentic religious life are not the words that we use to describe our religious experiences, but those experiences themselves. I do not assert that beneath the infinitely varied expressions of religious experience around the globe lies an unchanging experiential core—the "essence of religion." There is no sharp distinction between the immediacy of experience and the interpretation one gives of that experience. What we sense is informed by what we believe; the sensual takes shape around concepts that we have learned and take for granted.

Yet I am persuaded by my own experience and my encounters with persons of many faiths (including generations of students, many from abroad, who have passed through my courses) that within all of us, regardless of religious or cultural identity, lies a touchstone of discernment that if faithfully heeded leads to lives of greater justice, compassion, humility, and joy. Friends call this capacity the "Inner Light" or the "Inward Teacher," and (citing the Gospel of John) have seen it as "the true light, which enlightens everyone." (John 1:9)[26] While orthodox Christians identify the Inner Guide as the Christ-Spirit or "Holy Ghost," uniquely linked to the Jesus of the Gospels, I regard this account as but one among many cultural constructs created to express a Source that lies beyond all concepts.

Any discussion of the vexing question of Christian universalism versus Christian exclusivism must come to terms with John 14:5-6: "Thomas said to him, 'Lord, we do not know where you are going. How can we know the way?' Jesus said to him, 'I am the way, and the truth, and the life. No one comes to the Father except through me.'" I believe that this passage can be understood without strain as compatible with Christian universalism. "Doubting Thomas" worries that when the physical Jesus is no longer present, Thomas will be unable to find his way to God. When Jesus says to him "I am the way, the truth and the life. No one comes to the Father except through me," does Jesus refer to the physical human presence whom Thomas now sees? Obviously not, since Jesus is reassuring Thomas that what Jesus now incarnates in physical form will still be available to Thomas when the physical body of Jesus is absent. But if the pronouns "I" and "me" do not refer to the physical body of Jesus, to what do they point? Do they name a spiritual personage who is exclusively identified with the Christian revelation? Or do they draw our attention to the sacred Inward Teacher that is present in all of us, regardless of religious and cultural tradition? In this reading, Jesus reassures Thomas that when Jesus is no longer physically present, the wisdom that he incarnates—"the true light, which enlightens *everyone*"[27]—will still be available to Thomas. Elaine Pagels, Professor of Religion at Princeton University and a widely-read historian of Christianity, draws upon her reading of the non-canonical *Gospel of Thomas* to affirm a similar interpretation: "The divine light Jesus embodied is shared by humanity, since we are all made 'in the image of God,' which is hidden within everyone, although most people remain unaware of its presence."[28]

The 18th-century Quaker abolitionist, John Woolman, affirmed this understanding:

> There is a principle which is pure, placed in the human mind, which in different places and ages hath different names; it is, however, pure and proceeds from God. It is

deep and inward, confined to no forms of religion nor excluded from any where the heart stands in perfect sincerity. In whomsoever this takes root and grows, of what nation soever, they become brethren in the best sense of that expression.[29]

Given our propensity to conflate the inner voice of wisdom with the confused desires of our small selves, to twist genuine insights toward self-serving ends, it is not surprising that institutional keepers of religious order seek to define and enforce the boundaries of correct belief, distilling the tenets of authentic confession into a uniform religious "loyalty oath." When religious orthodoxy is co-opted by political authorities, this temptation to codify and enforce "true belief" becomes virtually irresistible.

Yet any effort to impose a tidy conceptual order upon the ineffability of Wonder and Mystery must fail. Worse, it diverts our reverence away from that which is most worthy of our devotion, redirecting that reverence toward verbal constructions, virtual "towers of Babel." The traditional Zen saying cautions, "You may use a finger to point at the moon—but do not mistake the finger for the moon." The opening lines of the *Tao Te Ching* aver that "The Tao which can be spoken of is not the eternal Tao; the name which can be named is not the eternal Name."[30] Insofar as orthodoxy diverts devotion away from Mystery toward dogma, it is inherently idolatrous.

If religious words are "fingers pointing at the moon," they are unavoidably colored by the unique character and location—cultural, geographical, social, political—of those who point. Attempting to impose a uniform system of sacred symbols and rituals upon this infinitely rich multiplicity of religious expressions is the height of religious imperialism. I will not rehearse the immense injustices (past and present) that have been perpetrated by such imperialism.[31] Suffice it to say that I rejoice in the varieties of "religious comfort food"; in sampling these piquant fares, I come to know myself better as a Quaker and a Christian. To suggest

that faithful practitioners of other traditions follow a "lesser revelation" than mine demeans not only them, but me as well.

Yet we eat good food not only to satisfy our palates but also
to nourish our bodies—and we know all too well that these crite-
ria do not always coincide: what tastes good may not be healthy
to ingest. Likewise with religious fare: that which satisfies religious impulse may ultimately be destructive to ourselves and to
others. Even as we seek a convivial accommodation between
religious traditions, we must retain our commitment to careful discernment of our own paths. As we seek to balance these
sometimes seemingly contrary considerations, we find that the
devil lies in the details. I do not offer a general solution to this
dilemma; instead, I am content to describe my own personal responses to it.

Pure Passion

What I sought after... was nothing but how to become
wholly God's. This made me resolve to give the all for the
all.

—Brother Lawrence[32]

I have been crucified in Christ, and it is no longer
I who live, but it is Christ who lives in me.

—Galatians 2:19-20

I am helped by the words of John Hick, quoted above: "The
function of religion... is to transform human existence from self-
centeredness to Reality-centeredness." I discern the ground of
this transformation in the central theme of this chapter: suspension of self-preoccupation and striving, yielding to direct awareness of one's present state in all of its immediate, concrete
particularity. I have felt the healing power of this full attention to
one's actual condition in many settings: in my own psychotherapeutic openings and in the rigorous progression of Twelve-Step

Programs; in the courageous candor of my students and the subsequent blossoming of their lives; in the suspension of striving that takes place in deep *zazen*; in yielding to "the wisdom from above" that frees me from violence; in the environmental activism that springs from our love of nature; and in the holy surrender of the Passion of Christ. When I no longer cling to coveted narratives about myself and instead open to the truth of my present state, my "heart stands in perfect sincerity"—and I open to the grace of a clarifying, liberating vision.

I term such moments "pure passion." "Pure" does not imply conformity to external moral standards, nor denial of the darkness within oneself. On the contrary, confrontation with that darkness—indeed, with *all* that I am—is the essence of such moments. In pure passion I suspend all willed actions and all habit energy, the compulsive reactions that obscure the present moment. Thus pure passion stands apart from fear and desire, which channel our energy into fanaticism or obsession and blind us to the larger import of our behavior. The estranged husband and father who, overcome with spiteful rage against his former wife, murders his own children and then himself, illustrates the potential evil of this self-enslavement. In contrast, pure passion relinquishes all partiality and awakens (in the words of Dorothy Soelle) to "that objectivity that issues in a complete giving over of oneself to what is being experienced."[33] Through abandonment of self-will, we awaken to a higher freedom than mere pursuit of preferences and taste the unencumbered peace of union with our heart's desire.

Compassion

If one completes the journey to one's own heart,
one will find oneself in the heart of everyone else.

—Father Thomas Keating[34]

When I acknowledge my own pain, I am much less squeamish about drawing nearer to yours.

—Marc Ian Barasch[35]

Why does surrender into the moment lead to compassion? Why does it not leave us in splendid isolation, content to bathe in our private bliss? The answer lies within the word "compassion," which means "to suffer with." When we drop resistance and become wholly vulnerable, the walls that we have erected to guard ourselves melt away—and we awaken to our intrinsic connections with one other, and with creation itself. Every person who cares for the suffering of another knows the heart connection that brings joy even in the midst of distress. To comfort a crying child; to listen sympathetically as a friend unburdens her troubled heart; to sit by the bedside of one who is dying while sharing the final flickers of his life, is to taste the blessing of uniting in love. As we open without reservation to our own lives, we also open to others; pure passion naturally converges upon compassion. Awareness enlarges beyond self-interest and awakens to what has been always true: in spite of our ignorance, our fears, our conflicts and struggles, we are inextricably interconnected.

Yet we know that when we encounter pain—our own, or that of others—we may not respond compassionately, but rather contract into a defensive posture and strike out against perceived threats. None of us manifests the radical openness to life that we see in great spiritual leaders such as Siddhartha Gautama or Jesus of Nazareth. Compassion in the presence of pain requires courage and discipline, and a recognition that we will always be on the path, never fully arriving. In the pithy words of Jack Kornfield, a beloved Buddhist teacher, "There is no state of enlightened retirement."[36]

What remains to us are the choices that we make on each step of our journeys.[37] Spiritual growth is a moment-to-moment challenge: encountering difficulty, shall we open or close?

Embrace or withdraw? Extend ourselves, or contract? We do both—sometimes more of one, sometimes more of the other, and often both simultaneously. Through centering silence we soften and become more resilient, more able to suspend our reactions and relax into the moment. Instead of focusing upon our own suffering, we awaken to a larger vision that lifts us from self-obsession into a more expansive, forgiving state. This is George Fox's counsel to the troubled Lady Claypoole[38]: do not obsess about your troubles, but rather, be aware of "the light that makes them manifest. For looking down at sin, and corruption, and distraction, you are swallowed up in it; but looking at the light that discovers them, you will see over them. That will give victory; and you will find grace and strength, and there is the first step of peace."[39]

Nowhere in Fox's lengthy letter to Lady Claypoole does he mention the crucifixion of Jesus, nor claim that a conventionally Christian interpretation of that event is required for redemption. The archetype of passion and redemption that Christians view through the prism of the Gospels transcends religious and cultural boundaries, appearing in many forms of healing growth around the world. The Spirit of Easter belongs to all.

I close by returning to the language of my own "religious comfort food," in the sincere hope that my readers will look beyond my own pointing finger to the moon itself and, using their own preferred religious language, give voice to what they see. Allowing for expansive, non-dogmatic interpretations of words like "Creator," "God," Christ," and "Divine," the contemporary religious writer whose language most fully captures my own inklings of spiritual devotion is Lloyd Lee Wilson, a Quaker who (like myself) comes out of the "Conservative" tradition of the Religious Society of Friends.[40] In a splendid little pamphlet, *Holy Surrender*,[41] Wilson contrasts "holy obedience" with "holy surrender":

> What does bring me peace is surrender: a relationship rather than a set of behaviors. One can be obedient at

arm's length, as it were—but surrender places us in an intimate relationship with our Creator. When I give up to God, when that relationship in all its grace and mercy shapes my life, there is a peace that passes beyond all understanding or describing. One way to think about surrender is as the desire to enter fully into the Body of Christ—to take my proper place in the Body, responding as fully and as quickly to the Divine thought as my own hand or tongue responds to my intention. This is a love relationship... .

It has been my experience that surrender to the Divine is not only our calling but also the occasion of the greatest, deepest, and most enduring joy I have known. Outward events may cause us pain, grief and sorrow, but nothing can touch or impair the deep joy that results from this continual intimacy with the Divine Love... .

The surrendered life, then, is one that loves God with the entirety of one's being, eliminating all that is not of God, and opening ever more fully to the true presence of God... . The surrendered life is one lived in the present reality of the Kingdom of God, while still physically located in this broken world. To love God "with all your heart, with all your soul, with all your mind, and with all your strength" is to hold nothing back.[42]

The third-century Desert Father, Anthony, is said to have remarked, "If you see that a young man is striving for heaven with his own will, grasp his feet and drag him down; for it will do him no good."[43] Looking back to August 1957, I now see that my feverish flight on waxen wings was driven not by healthy aspiration, but by eagerness to escape a self-engrossed and troubled life. It has taken me a lifetime to reverse this flight, to discover that the true journey of healing and wholeness leads not into the distant skies—but inward, into my own heart. The joy of pure passion comes not through escape but through willing surrender... to Ultimate Mystery, and to a life of service that flows naturally out of that surrender.

Part II:

ILLUMINATION

CHAPTER FOUR

LIVING PEACE

Love your enemies, do good to those who hate you,
bless those who curse you, pray for those who abuse you.
If anyone strikes you on the cheek, offer the other also... .
Do unto others as you would have them do unto you.

—*Luke 6:27-31*

Personal Struggles

"Slug" Malone is younger and smaller than me, perhaps eight years old to my nine, but he knows that he can attack me with impunity. Forbidden by my Quaker parents from fighting—even in self-defense—I have become an easy mark for every bully at my rural elementary school. Inside the schoolhouse I am usually safe, but recess time is a daily nightmare: I must choose between being attacked or running away.

My parents draw their convictions first from the New Testament (especially the Sermon on the Mount) and then from the Quaker Peace Testimony. Having lost a younger brother in World War II, my father has resolved that his son will walk a

69

more peaceful path. A dutiful child, I comply, even as I beg for permission to defend myself. One evening after I make a particularly desperate appeal to my mother, she seems to relent. The next morning when Slug again attacks me, I swing wildly in the direction of his face. He retreats, cries, throws a rock— and never bothers me again.

Despite this apparent vindication of violent self-defense, I am enthralled by the moral beauty of Jesus' teachings. To love one's enemies, to return good for evil, to bless those who taunt me seems an admirable and heroic path. Even as I seethe with rancor, I fall in love with love and cultivate a generous life.

Entering a Quaker boarding school brings relief. I find myself in an educational environment where we are expected to treat one another with respect and kindness. Yet even here, students are not always true to these values; subtle spite can still make my life miserable. Feeing rejected and shamed by older boys, I devise a strategy to "do good to those who hate you," by secretly performing good deeds to benefit them. When they confront me and ask point-blank whether I am their secret benefactor I lie, denying any responsibility.

My clandestine acts are curiously comforting. I act partly out of pride, refusing to let unkindness derail my determination to be loving. But I am moved by another insight as well: retaliation will only submerge me in greater conflict and misery, whereas when I muster a generous response, the cycle of hostility lifts—and I feel better about myself and my life. Despite lingering rancor, I find solace in Jesus' message of love and healing.

When I turn 18, I register under the Selective Service Act, then apply for status as a conscientious objector, which is readily granted by my draft board. Yet even at the Quaker-related college that I attend, I am still occasionally overtaken by violence. In my first year I somehow incur the scorn and fury of some older male students, who force their way into my dormitory room and attack me. Though I do not strike back, I at first resist; when that proves futile, I drop to the floor in a fetal position. They trash my room and beat my curled body, then storm out. Later one of them berates me for not fighting back. I say nothing. I come away from that encounter with a curious sense of triumph.

Many years later when my son is tormented by schoolyard bullies, I revisit these issues. Remembering my childhood trauma, I urge him to seek peaceful solutions whenever possible—but do not insist that he refrain from defending himself. Still, the message of nonviolence seems to prevail. As his 18th birthday approaches, I help him to create a file to support a request for C.O. status, should the draft be reinstated.

Never again have I suffered actual physical violence. In this, I am indeed fortunate: countless others regularly endure abuse. Yet I remain vulnerable to emotional distress. Often sensitive and thin-skinned, I struggle more with hurt feelings than with physical pain and am jarred by rudeness, insensitivity, or malice. It is a continual challenge to be kind, yet stand up for myself and others.

Neither Jesus nor George Fox counsel me be a doormat, passively absorbing abuse. The love to which they call me is not weak; it does not ignore cruelty and injustice. On the contrary, the messages of nonviolence, love, and forgiveness that I find in the Bible and in Quaker testimonies ask more of me—more courage, more strength, more discipline—than are required by acquiescence or retaliation. I can be fiercely self-critical when I fall short (as I often do) of these high expectations. Yet self-recrimination is also emotional violence. If I am to forgive others, I must forgive myself as well.

Beneath the small melodramas of my life lies a deep yearning to live into the values that I hold most dear. For many years I struggled to live those values by sheer effort, trying to force my life into conformity with my ideals. I do not discount these efforts; on balance, I have been better for them. If I cannot always be pure in heart, I can at least do the right thing. Even when done through gritted teeth, generous actions are preferable to cruelty or indifference. But at a deeper level, I realize the futility of my strivings. I cannot by will-power remake myself into the stuff of my dreams; I cannot compel myself to love.

Living in Virtue

> God is love, and those who abide in love abide in God, and God abides in them.... . (T)here is no fear in love, but perfect love casts out fear.
> —I John 4:16-18

In April 1651,[1] George Fox was approached by military recruiters who sought to make him a captain in Cromwell's army. Accused of blasphemy, Fox had been imprisoned in the Derby House of Corrections; his six-month term was nearing completion. At age 27, Fox was already recognized as a fearless preacher and a "discerning spirit."[2] The recruiters sweetened their offer by offering release from prison and by compliments regarding Fox's bravery.

Fox flatly refused, however, declaring that he "lived in the virtue of that life and power that took away the occasion of all wars, and (he) knew from whence all wars did rise, from the lust according to James' doctrine."[3] Supposing that Fox might be affecting false modesty, the recruiters pressed their offer, saying that they made it "in love and kindness because of (Fox's) virtue." Fox's blunt reply was not calculated to ingratiate: "I told them that if that were their love and kindness I trampled it under my feet." Furious, the recruiters saw to it that Fox was sent to Derby dungeon, "a lousy, stinking low place in the ground without any bed." Fox remained incarcerated in Derby for another six months—almost doubling his original sentence.

Assuming the accuracy of Fox's account (recorded decades after the incident), his stout refusal of military service in 1651 marks the first appearance of what has become known as the Quaker Peace Testimony. (Another decade would elapse before the 1661 Declaration, often celebrated as the basis of Friends' opposition to war.) Fox explained his refusal of military service by citing a short book from the New Testament, the Epistle of James. Yet Fox's justification was not doctrinal but experiential; instead of arguing for an orthodox interpretation of scripture, Fox claimed to live in an exalted spiritual state which liberated him from the realm of wars, strife, and bloody conflict. The implication that he was spiritually superior to the men who spoke to him undoubtedly inflamed their fury.

The Source of Wars and Fightings

What is the state that Fox claimed for himself? The primary concern of the Epistle of James is not with politics or public policy, but with personal conduct. It is a caution against anger and a call to faithfulness, patience, and discipline:

(L)et every man be swift to hear, slow to speak, slow to wrath: for the wrath of man worketh not the righteousness of God.... (T)he wisdom that is from above is first pure, then peaceable, gentle, and easy to be entreated, full of mercy and good fruits, without partiality, and without hypocrisy. And the fruit of righteousness is sown in peace of them that make peace.

From whence come wars and fightings among you? Come they not hence, even of your lusts that war in your members? Ye lust, and have not: ye kill, and desire to have, and cannot obtain: ye fight and war, yet ye have not.... Ye ask, and receive not, because ye ask amiss, that ye may consume it upon your lusts.

—The General Epistle of James, 1:19-20, 3:17-4:3 KJV[4]

War and conflict arise from cravings that are contrary to "the righteousness of God." Until we have yielded to the Spirit, we are torn by competing desires and tempted by what does not truly satisfy. Thus we quarrel, using force and violence to gain our ends.

A Redemptive Vision

The first step of peace is to stand still in the light.

—*George Fox*[5]

We find redemption by standing in the Light and opening to Truth. Through a painful yet cleansing process, we see ourselves clearly—and realize our unity with one another. Abiding in God, we know that God abides in us. Love banishes fear. Anxiety is replaced by confidence, courage, and joy; we find our prophetic voice and are free to act boldly in the world.

Fox would later call this process "the royal law of love."[6] When he declared that he "lived in the virtue of that life and power that took away the occasion of all wars," Fox was reporting the fruits of his own spiritual discipline: he knew from his own experience that the solution to conflict lies in spiritual surrender and self-transcendence. By 1651 Fox could speak of such surrender with personal authority. His years of seeking, depression, and despair had culminated in the great openings of 1647 and 1648, when he experienced a radical transformation: "When all my hopes... in all men were gone, so that I had nothing outwardly to help me, nor could tell what to do, then, Oh then, I heard a voice which said, 'There is one, even Christ Jesus, that can speak to thy condition,' and when I heard it my heart did leap for joy."[7]

From this moment of redemption onward, Fox's "zeal in the pure knowledge of God and of Christ alone" grew; "the Lord did gently lead me along, and did let me see his love, which was endless and eternal." Turning from reliance upon earthly voices to "Christ, who hath the key, and opened the door of light and life unto me,"[8] Fox found a new life of "liberty and freedom."[9] "My sorrows and troubles began to wear off and tears of joy dropped from me, so that I could have wept night and day with tears of joy to the Lord, in humility and brokenness of heart."[10] As "the Lord's power brake forth more and more wonderfully," Fox's spiritual openings rose to a passionate pitch:

> Now was I come up in spirit through the flaming sword into the paradise of God. All things were new, and all the creation gave another smell unto me than before, beyond what words can utter. I knew nothing but pureness, and innocency, and righteousness, being renewed up into the image of God by Christ Jesus, so that I say I was come up to the state of Adam which he was in before he fell. ... I was immediately taken up in spirit, to see into another or more steadfast state than Adam's in innocency, even into a state in Christ Jesus, that should never fall.[11]

This vision was to guide Fox for the remainder of his life. Humble and broken before God, he was outspoken in the world, denouncing evil and hypocrisy with the passion of a prophet. Repeated imprisonments did not quell his zeal. Finally released from prison in October 1651, he resumed a bold public ministry that provoked the fury of authorities and their sympathizers, often leading to severe beatings and abuse.

An incident of such abuse occurred at Ulverston in mid-1652, not long after Fox had first met Margaret Fell at Swarthmoor Hall. "Moved to go again to Ulverston steeplehouse where there was abundance of professors, and priests, and friendly people to hear me,"[12] Fox soon infuriated the preacher, as well as a justice of the peace and many others who were present. The resulting chaos was a stern challenge to Fox's claim that he was above "wars and strife." Assuming that his account is accurate, Fox passed this test with flying colors:

> Then the rude people said to the Justice, "Give him

us!" and he did. So of a sudden all the people in the steeplehouse were in an outrage and an uproar, that they fell
upon me in the steeplehouse before his face, with staves
and fists and books, and knocked me down and kicked me
and trampled upon me... . And at last the Justice... led me
out of the steeplehouse and put me into the hands of four
officers and constables, and bid them whip me and put
me out of the town. And they led me about a quarter of a
mile, some taking hold by my collar and some by the arms
and shoulders and shook me by the head, and some by the
hands, and dragged me through mire and dirt and water... .

And when they had led me to the common moss... the
constables took me and gave me a wisk over the shoulders with their willow rods, and so thrust me amongst the
rude multitude which then fell upon me with their hedge
stakes and clubs and staves and beat me as hard as ever
they could strike on my head and arms and shoulders, and
it was a great while before they beat me down and mazed
me, and at last I fell down upon the wet common. There I
lay a pretty space, and when I recovered myself again, and
saw myself lying on a watery common, and all the people standing about me, I lay a little still, and the power of
the Lord sprang through me, and the eternal refreshings
refreshed me, that I stood up again in the eternal power
of God and stretched out my arms amongst them all, and
said again with a loud voice, "Strike again, here is my arms
and my head and my cheeks." And there was a mason, a
rude fellow, a professor called, he gave me a blow with all
his might just a-top of my hand, as it was stretched out,
with his walking rule-staff. And my hand and arm was so
numbed and bruised that I could not draw it in unto me
again, but it stood out as it was. Then the people cried
out, "He hath spoiled his hand, for ever having any use if it
more." The skin was struck off my hand and a little blood

came, and I looked at it in the love of God, and I was in the love of God to them all that had persecuted me.[13]

Fox was not the only one who had been attacked. Returning to Swarthmoor Hall, he "found it turned into a veritable hospital as servants scurried around to bind the wounds of the injured."[14] He reported that "my body and arms were yellow, black, and blue with the blows and bruises that I received amongst them that day."[15] After similar incidents in the next fortnight, including an assassination attempt by a man with a pistol (the firearm did not discharge) and another mob beating that left Fox so sore that "when I was in bed I could turn me no more than a sucking child, I was so bruised," Fox was asked about his persecution by Judge Fell, the sympathetic husband of Margaret Fell. He replied that his abusers "could not do otherwise, they were in such a spirit."[16]

Though described in unusual detail, the Ulverson incident is far from unique. On many occasions throughout his lifetime of public ministry, Fox endured not only angry denunciations and verbal abuse, but also physical attacks—to say nothing of his years of incarceration, often under the harshest conditions. Fox's typical response to such personal challenges was a defiant re-assertion of his ministry and stout refusal to engage in physical self-defense or retaliation. A 1656 incident in Cornwall that took place behind closed doors encapsulates Fox's fortitude: "and he comes (sic) upon me and struck me with both his hands and clapped his leg behind me and would fain have thrown me down, but he could not. But I stood stiff and still and let him strike."[17]

The Voices of Quaker Women

Unalterably convinced by her encounter with Fox, Margaret Fell soon became a courageous public voice and nurturing mother of the fledgling Quaker movement. As Larry Ingle notes, "Margaret Fell's rapid rise... accurately mirrored the qualities of a remarkable person."[18] Mother of seven children (an eighth would come a year later), she managed her family's large estate when her husband was away. Fell arranged for copying and circulation of key writings by Friends and became the de facto treasurer of the movement. Her "undaunted zeal"[19] in speaking out on behalf of Friends (she was named by hostile informants as the "chief maintainer" of the sect in the area[20]) eventually led to her own imprisonment.

Margaret Fell early recognized the nonviolent spirit of Quakerism. In 1653, barely a year after she had first met George Fox, she wrote a scathing letter to Judge John Archer, who had sentenced numerous Friends to prison, declaring to him that "Thou hast exercised thy cruelty upon a harmless people, that will offer violence to no man, nor wrong any man."[21] Elsa Glines cites these words as "a very early statement of the peace principle which was not generally established among Quakers until 1660."[22]

Early support by Quaker women for the Peace Testimony came from other quarters as well. In a 1653 epistle, Agnes Wilkenson urged "all who handle a sword and take up carnal weapons... to strip yourself naked of all your carnal weapons and take unto you the sword of the Spirit, for the Lord is coming to judge men."[23] Later in the decade, Quaker women were prominent in Friends' public testimony against the paying of tithes, which they linked to times of war. One broadside signed by more than 350 Quaker women from Cheshire begins with the declaration that Christ brings an end to "Tithes in the War" and "ends the War and makes Peace on earth... and destroys the Devil, the cause of War and strifes... whereby he brings Peace on earth and reconciliation with God."[24] In 1660, Margaret Fell delivered a paper to the king and to both houses of Parliament with a fuller statement of the Peace Testimony:

We are a people that follow after those things that
make for peace, love and unity; it is our desire that others'

feet may walk in the same, and do deny and bear our testimony against all strife, and wars, and contentions that come from the lusts that war in the members, that war in the soul... and love and desire the good of all.[25]

Declaring Against War

All bloody principles and practices, as to our own particulars, we utter deny... .

—George Fox[26]

Springing from personal experience, tested in the fire of mob violence, the Peace Testimony assumed over time a more public, corporate profile. Fox's early rejection of a position in the army was couched in the first person singular: "I told them I lived in the virtue of that life and power that took away the occasion of all wars," and "I told them I was brought off from outward wars... . I told them I was dead to (becoming a soldier)."[27] Later statements of the Peace Testimony are more generalized declarations on behalf of all Friends. This shift from personal spiritual testimony to a public, corporate statement was hastened by the need for a "public relations" response to unfolding threats to the Quaker movement.

The first of these responses was Fox's 1655 letter to Oliver Cromwell, then Lord Protector and commander of the New Model Army. Cromwell became concerned that Fox and the rapidly-growing Quaker movement might pose a military threat to public order. He summoned Fox for reassurance. Fox was only too glad to oblige. In a letter to Cromwell, Fox abjures "the carrying or drawing of any carnal sword against any, or against thee, Oliver Cromwell, or any man," declaring that he "is sent to stand a witness against all violence... and to turn people... from the occasion of the war... . My weapons are not carnal but spiritual... therefore with a carnal weapon I do not fight."[28]

The Need for the Sword

Fox does, however, assure Cromwell of the need for coercive force to maintain public order ("the magistrate bears not the sword in vain," echoing Romans 13:4)—and acknowledges Cromwell's proper role in "cleansing the land of evil doers." In keeping with his declaration of 1651, Fox claims for himself (and, by implication, for Friends) a higher spiritual calling that repudiates all violence and carnal weapons. As Larry Ingle notes, in Fox's letter to Cromwell he does not endorse pacifism as it is now understood. "While he was personally opposed to participating in war, he recognized and accepted the authority of the state to use the sword."[29] "Fox... repeatedly recognized... that a magistrate who bore a weapon might permissibly use it in a just cause. He did not deny, and would never deny, the right of a nation's rulers to wield weapons in the defense of a just cause."[30] Fox believed that Quakers showed the way to a new covenant of peace in which the sword would no longer be necessary; until that covenant was complete, however, lawful worldly rulers were bound to use the sword as "a terror to the evil doers who act contrary to the light of the Lord Jesus Christ."[31]

In a world of injustice and violence, Friends' primary responsibility was to follow a higher path: to serve as living models, showing the way to a Christ-embodied life. This theme is eloquently stated in one of the most beloved passages from Fox's writings, dictated while he was imprisoned in Launceston in Cornwall in 1656:

> And this is the word of the Lord God to you all, and a charge to you all in the presence of the living God, be patterns, be examples in all countries, places, islands, nations, wherever you come; that your carriage and life may preach among all sorts of people, and to them.[32]

The first decade of charismatic Quakerism, marked by extraordinarily rapid growth (according to Ingle, by 1659 some thirty thousand had become Friends[33]) would soon be overtaken by tumultuous events that threatened the very existence of the movement. As the political environment deteriorated following the death of Cromwell in 1658, Quakers came under greater suspicion for contributing to public disorder and challenging legitimate authority. Igniting this volatile mix, in early 1661[34] a small band of revolutionaries called the Fifth Monarchists staged a quixotic rebellion against the reign of the new King, Charles II. They were quickly overcome and destroyed—but Friends were suspected of complicity.

The 1661 Declaration

In response to this crisis, Fox and some eleven other male Quakers (no women were asked to participate) drafted a public statement denying involvement by Friends in the rebellion, and affirming in more sweeping language than ever before, Friends' refusal to rely upon "carnal weapons." This document, the "Declaration from the Harmless and Innocent People of God called Quakers," sought to protect Friends from false accusations and unjust persecution. It was not formally approved by any body of Friends other than those who drafted it. Still, the Declaration has come to be viewed with pride by Quakers as the *locus classicus* of the Friends Peace Testimony, gaining what Quaker scholar Chuck Fager calls canonical status among Friends.[35]

Fager points out that the Declaration is not an unqualified endorsement of universal pacifism, as contemporary Friends often suppose it to be. It does not oppose all use of force; in fact (following Romans 13:1-7) the 1661 Declaration endorses "the power ordained of God for the punishment of evil-doers" when exercised by legitimate authorities. The Declaration claims for Friends a special spiritual status that lifts them (unlike most others) above the use of carnal weapons; the law and the sword were made not for the righteous, but "for sinners and transgressors, to keep them down."[36]

The 1661 Declaration claims that unlike the Fifth Monarchists, Friends have been "redeemed... from this unrighteous world, and... are not of it, but are heirs of a world of which there is no end.... . Our weapons are spiritual, and not carnal... therefore we cannot learn war any more." The claim of innocence and righteousness is repeatedly invoked: "This we can say to all the world, we have wronged no man, we have used no force nor violence against any man: we have been found in no plots, nor guilty of sedition."

As Fager notes, the often-quoted line from early in the Declaration, "We utterly deny all outward wars and strife" is a misleading condensation of the original, which reads, "All bloody principles and practices, as to our own particulars, we utterly deny... ." This is not a flat prohibition of outward wars and strife, but rather a claim that Quakers ("the innocent... babes of Christ...") occupy an elevated spiritual status: a harmless, nonviolent people, they would never engage in the seditious acts of which they were accused.

Is the 1661 Declaration merely a desperate public relations ploy, a disingenuous attempt to deflect persecution? No. Despite its topical political origins, the Declaration is consistent with Fox's statements of 1651 and 1655, discussed above. All in turn hearken back to the substance of Fox's great spiritual openings of 1647 and 1648, in which he was "come up to the state of Adam which he was in before he fell," and then "taken up in spirit, to see another or more steadfast state than Adam's... in innocency, even into a state in Christ Jesus, that should never fall."[37] When we have truly awakened to the Christ within, we are no longer slaves to our lusts and experience "the wisdom that is from above... full of mercy and good fruits... And the fruit of righteousness is sown in peace of them that make peace." To experience this great blessing is to become dead to wars and fightings; once we have experienced such grace, we cannot learn war any more. Liberation from wars and strife requires spiritual surrender; only when we live in the virtue of the life and power of God may we find peace.

Testimonies and Principles

The Lord... opened it to me how that people and professors... fed upon words, and fed one another with words, but trampled upon the life, and... the blood of the Son of God... and they lived in their airy notions talking of him.

—George Fox[38]

(Early Friends) were changed... themselves before they went about to change others. Their hearts were rent as well as their garments, and they knew the power and work of God upon them... . The bent and stress of their ministry was conversion to God, regeneration and holiness, not schemes of doctrines and verbal creeds.

—William Penn[39]

Fox's qualified endorsement of the sword in the 1661 Declaration will disappoint those who favor universal pacifism. Yet the Peace Testimony did not originate as a universal principle that is binding on everyone. Throughout most of the history of the Religious Society of Friends, the Peace Testimony has been understood rather as the specific expression of changed lives, the fruit of spiritual transformation.

What is the distinction between testimonies and principles? Personal testimony in a court of law is a report of one's own experience. Speculation and sweeping generalization are out of order; one must state only that which one directly knows. Friends' testimonies reflect a similar understanding—not abstract generalizations, but the fruit of faithful lives. In contrast, abstract principles are presumed to stand above subjective experience, free of the vagaries of particular history and unique circumstance, and may be adopted through an act of will by reasonable persons everywhere, regardless of how they have actually lived.

The appeal of universal, abstract principles was enhanced by the flowering of the European Enlightenment in the 18th Century. Truth was seen as transcending culture; it is identical for all rational beings and independent of the experiential history of individuals. Severed from subjectivity and personal narrative, the affirmation of universal principles is bloodless and detached— a passion of the mind, perhaps, but not of the heart. In recent years this model of truth has come under sustained attack, culminating in the postmodern and deconstructionist critiques of recent decades.[40] Still, as children of the 20th and 21st Centuries, we are unavoidably subject to its allure; we crave the apparent security of universal, abstract truth.

For 17th-century Friends, however, spiritual truth was not an intellectual judgment, but rather an effusion of direct experience; it gave voice to the passion of souls that had submitted to the Light. Quaker testimonies arose out of this transforming fire; they were records of the shared experience of nakedness before the inner Christ. In the words of Wilmer Cooper, "The testimonies are the moral and ethical fruit of the inward leading of the Spirit... . Testimonies are... outward expressions that reflect the inward experience of divine guidance."[41]

If words and intellectual judgments serve to direct our experience toward the Light, they have heuristic value; standing by themselves, however, they cannot sustain us. Feeding ourselves with words, we trample upon the life—and fall short of regeneration and holiness.

Principle Integrity vs. Deep Authenticity

From the distinction between testimonies and principles arise contrasting models of integrity. To assert a general principle calls for a certain sort of consistency: what I assert as a rule of good conduct, I must strive to live by or stand accused of hypocrisy. I should (we now say) *walk the talk*. Principle integrity is top-heavy: first a judgment of the mind, then the conforming action.[42]

In contrast, Friends' testimonies are not judgments of the mind but voices from the heart. True insight comes not in the form of a doctrine, dogma, or principle, but in the stark recognition of the condition of my life. Submitting to this moment, I act accordingly. We must first live Truth before we may declare it; Fox says, "profess no more than you are."[43] Quaker integrity is not mere logical consistency, but deep authenticity: not merely conforming one's behavior with one's professed principles, but speaking what one has become, *talking the walk*.

If I endorse a principle of goodness and try to adhere to it, I engage in earnest self-management, imitating my professed ideal. Such efforts inevitably fail. I cannot by my own efforts perfect myself; I cannot will myself into a state of grace. St. Paul confesses, "When I want to do what is good, evil lies close at hand. For I delight in the law of God in my inmost self, but I see in my members another law,... making me captive to the law of sin." In contrast, "all things work together for good for those who love God." (Romans 7:21-23, 8:28) Yet when I yield to the Inward Teacher, right action flows naturally.

Principle Pacifism
vs. Testimony Pacifism

The Peace Testimony exemplifies not *principle pacifism* but *testimony pacifism*. It is not a philosophical generalization to be affirmed by intellectual judgment (as if one were endorsing the platform of a political party); rather, it is a confession of spiritual surrender and the fruit of that surrender. George Fox was dead to becoming a soldier because he was alive to the God of love. If my profession of the Peace Testimony is authentic, I must know in my body and being "the wisdom from above (that) is first pure, then peaceable, gentle, willing to yield, full of mercy and good fruits, without a trace of partiality or hypocrisy." Abiding in God, I abide in love.

Few persons anywhere can honestly claim to know intimately in each moment that they rest in the womb of God. More likely, we yearn for such peace but see it as a distant heaven, far removed from our present experience. Yet the message of Quakerism—and indeed, of Christianity itself—is that such blessedness lies not in some distant place and time, but rests within us even now, and can be known by opening to our own depths, to the Light within. Indeed, hints and glimmerings of the Light always flicker in the recesses of our consciousness, calling us to give ourselves to them. For most Friends, the affirmation of the Peace Testimony will be an act of faith sustained by traces of intuitive knowing "through a glass darkly," but with the hope of knowing more fully in God's time.

When the Peace Testimony loses its ground in the direct experience of transformed lives and becomes principle pacifism—an intellectual judgment, bolstered by emotion—it does not lose all force or value. Those who are guided not by direct experience of divine grace but by philosophical concepts of justice, nonviolence, and peace may do honorable and necessary work. Still, without its spiritual ground, the Peace Testimony is profoundly weakened. It becomes merely a Peace Principle—one partisan position among others, subject to debate, contention, and counterexample. When I act "on principle" without grounding in the Spirit, I am oblivious to the present moment. With eyes fixed on an ideal horizon, I overlook what is beneath my feet. Because I do not taste and feel the inner peace of God's love, I may fall into acrimony and divisiveness, giving the lie to my professed ideal. Peace becomes an abstract goal to be achieved by any means.

Asserting principle pacifism, I am vulnerable to hypothetical wrangles: "You say you are a pacifist—but what would you do if someone attacked your loved ones?" Testimony pacifism relieves me from these fruitless fantasies. Standing in a wordless conviction of the Light, I need no argument. To those who pose hypothetical "what if" challenges, my honest answer is "I cannot say, until I am in such a situation. I can only hope to be faithful and open to my leadings, if the circumstance arises." If I commit to a principle, I am logically bound to follow my professed rule regardless of circumstances. But when I do not endorse a general principle, but rather testify to my experience of the love of God, I adapt to what love requires.

Because it rests in experience of the love of God, testimony pacifism is serene, acting with the assurance of divine presence even in chaotic circumstances. When that assurance is lost and opposition to war becomes a rootless principle affirmed by well-meaning minds, the grace of Divine providence is obscured and forgotten, replaced by human striving: "It all depends on me!" In principle pacifism, "peace work" may arise not from love but from anger and desperation. Such efforts are likely to be ineffective or even counterproductive. When I am tormented by fearful, angry thoughts—whether about the causes of violence and war, or anything else—I cannot see straight. I cannot discern alternative options. My creativity withers. I become strident and obsessive. True empathy is blocked, and I project my frustrations upon what I see as an evil enemy, beyond the pale.

In contrast, testimony pacifism draws its strength from the experience of God's presence. As I grow in my willingness to trust this experience and live from it, I am increasingly able to accept what comes. Declining to inflict my own pain upon others, I bear my cross and am freed to respond to hatred with love.

The distinction between testimonies and principles applies not only to Friends' witness on peace, but also to the whole of Quaker faith and practice. What might be called *principle*

Quakerism—a body of attractive values regarding peace, simplicity, integrity, community, and so on—is a free-floating belief system that has lost its roots in transforming spiritual experience, and thus lacks vitality and dynamic power. In contrast, *testimony Quakerism* is the authentic fruit of the inner Christ, that of God within one's own heart—the source from which all else flows. Though one may first be drawn to Quakers through the appeal of their apparent principles, one grows into the fullness of life as a Friend when one knows those principles as personal testimonies, arising from the power and work of God.

As a boy I struggled to manifest the teachings of Jesus in my own life. While I was powerfully drawn to those teachings, they were for me merely idealistic principles rather than true testimonies growing out of my own spiritual experience. Still, my earnest desire to realize them in my life led me to a spiritual practice that opened me to a more intimate encounter with the Light. As my spiritual life slowly deepens, the strain of conforming to idealistic principles is eased, giving way to a comforting Presence that softens my struggles and gladdens my heart.

Thus the contrast between principles and testimonies may be overdrawn. We need not choose between an arid adoption of abstract philosophical principles on the one hand, and a blind submission to religious passion on the other. Religious discipline begins with adoption of precepts of right and wrong, good and bad, as defined by a faith tradition, and—if the tradition is sound, and the discipline is faithful—moves to a deeper experience of the sustaining Spirit disclosed by the tradition. The interplay of principle and testimony is a dynamic dialectic, in which heuristic principle points to the root of religious truth, even as personal testimony increasingly infuses principle with life and blood.[44]

Seeking Peace

It is in vain that you rise up early and go late to rest, eating the bread of anxious toil; for he gives sleep to his beloved.
— Psalm 127:2

In our hasty desire for the fruit of right social order, we have neglected the Root from which all good fruit springs.
— Lloyd Lee Wilson[45]

The Peace Testimony arose from an awakened spiritual state that (as Fox knew) was not shared by everyone. Early Friends sought to reduce "wars and fightings"; indeed, they hoped to usher in a new age of liberation from all bloody principles and practices. But they saw the path to realizing such a prophetic vision as first spiritual, and only then political, a path of regeneration and holiness. Just as Fox acknowledged the duty of legitimate political authorities to maintain public order by the use of force, so most Friends in subsequent generations have acknowledged the need for magistrates or police officers to enforce the law and maintain order.[46] Friends have spoken out against abuses within the system of criminal justice, seeking rehabilitation and fair treatment of incarcerated criminals.[47] Many Quakers today wrestle with the question of whether military police action to protect the innocent may sometimes be preferable to a total rejection of any use of coercive force.

Maintenance of public order, the protection of the innocent, respect for life and property, all ideally arise spontaneously from a willing submission to the Christ within. Even those who turn a blind eye to the Light in their own conscience may sometimes be "brought off from subjection" when their self-deception is pointed out to them. But not everyone is willing to listen. Those who refuse to heed their own Inner Teacher may require external constraints. Until heaven is established upon earth, the power of the magistrate will be necessary. Anarchism—the rejection of governmental authority and all coercive means to maintain that authority—is not and has never been a Quaker testimony.

Voicing Unpopular Truth

Fox and early Friends enthusiastically denounced the faithlessness and hypocrisy, injustice and greed that they saw around them. Such denunciations were sometimes acrimonious, reflecting petty fears and rancor. Historically, most Friends were—and today, most Friends are—far from saintly. Still, a true prophetic voice does not arise from the reactions of the ego, but from a clear discernment of Truth, grounded not in fear but in love. It may be sharp but not shrill, direct but not demeaning.

The brave declaration of unpopular truth is for me an especially difficult dimension of faithfulness. I know that my wisdom is limited, and I fear offending others. When I speak unpopular truth, the reaction has often been unpleasant for me. My hesitation is reinforced by recognizing that much of what passes as courageous truth-telling is mere polemical rant, indulgence of an outraged ego rather than the voice of divine inspiration. Because I abhor such bluster, I rationalize my silence.

The most difficult step is also the most basic: courageous submission to the truth of my life, without inflicting my pain upon others. Resolute, unflinching recognition of who I am—with all of my small gifts and large failings, my shortcomings and self-deceptions—is the cleansing fire, the utterly humbling submission to the Light that destroys my delusions and awakens me to divine grace, awakening the recognition that I am loved just as I am. Without standing in the Light, any theological reassurance I receive is a mere airy notion, lacking redemptive power—and my efforts at peacemaking are merely earnest posturing, an attempt (as Lloyd Lee Wilson writes) to manifest fruit without grounding in the Root.

Retreat and Outreach

Should I then turn all of my energies inward, seeking to purify my inner life and deepen my faithfulness before I act to promote peace and justice? Should I (as is often said in facile tones) "make peace in myself before I make peace in the world"? Should I put the world on hold while I work only on myself?

There are certainly times when retreat is necessary. When I am tired, or torn, or distracted and confused, my effectiveness as an agent of change is compromised, and I may need to withdraw in order to seek my own healing and renewal. But when my retreat becomes an ongoing path of avoidance, an excuse for maintaining personal comfort rather than faithfulness to the Light, my spiritual life becomes narcissistic and precious. I indulge in New Age Quakerism: insulated by affluence from real suffering and injustice, I focus upon a purely inward quest, rationalizing my distaste for public witness by skepticism regarding the effectiveness of work for peace and justice.

Just as there is an appropriate balance for each individual of inner work and outreach, of quiet retreat and activist engagement, so within each community of Friends, there is an appropriate division of labor that arises naturally when individuals are true to their own specific gifts and callings. I have sometimes described myself as having the heart of a contemplative and the conscience of an activist, causing me to feel torn between the inner path of renewal and holiness, and the outward path of doing justice and mercy. In thinking about this tension, I have been helped by vocal ministry of a sensitive Friend who feels the same conflicting tugs upon her heart. She shared an image of a community of seekers at the edge of the ocean, holding hands. Some stand solidly on shore, providing anchor; others venture into the shallows, providing essential linkage, while yet others brave the swelling, crashing waves. All are joined by hands of love and support. Roles shift with time: those burned out by too much buffeting and exposure may retreat for a time, while others who have gathered energy and insight on shore may venture boldly into the waves. Throughout such dynamic shifts, the work of peace and justice is most effective when it is guided by corporate discernment in a loving community. When this linkage of mutual support is broken, those in the swirling tumult of the ocean may lose their bearings and be swept away, their struggles overwhelmed by more powerful forces—while those on the shore may be tempted to turn their backs upon an engaged life and huddle around small campfires for warmth, far from the roiling seas. To sustain both inwardness and outreach, we need the support of each other.[48]

I must guard against the illusion that I cannot begin to promote peace and justice around me until I am fully realized as a spiritual being. As many stories in scripture and in our own experience attest, those who make a difference, who do God's work in the world, are themselves profoundly imperfect, deeply flawed individuals who are nevertheless committed to Spirit-led transformation. What spiritual awakening brings to my social activism is not moral perfection, but freedom from fear, and thus a more joyful pursuit of a better world. Surrendering my heart and mind to the Light empowers me to act in grace, to extend my energies beyond what I formerly could do—because I act not from my own weakness, but from the strength of the Spirit. The prophetic voice is powerful—clear, confident, courageous—because it is the voice of a soul that has found its true home in God.

In summary:

- **The heart of the Quaker Peace Testimony is an awakening to the presence of the God of love.** Without transformation by this limitless, blessed reality, my profession of peace remains an airy notion, an attempt to manifest the fruit without the Root.

- **The degree to which I can offer a genuinely nonviolent, loving response to war, hatred, and injustice**

depends upon the depth of my spiritual discipline, the measure of Light in my conscience. My first challenge is to manifest the Peace Testimony in my own life: to become more loving and forgiving.

- **The path to peace is through acceptance of my own pain**—*not* acquiescing in abuse, injustice, and evil, but rather, accepting without retaliation what follows upon courageous witnessing for peace and justice.

- **Spirit-led peace and justice work is joyful, not despairing. I promote peace best by spreading good news, not bad.** When my efforts to promote peace and justice become anxious and despairing, I have lost the redemptive, joyful vision from which the original Peace Testimony sprang.

- **The Peace Testimony is a *testimony*, not a general philosophical principle or a statement of public policy.** It was not intended by George Fox to be a universal rule that all should follow, regardless of their circumstances and spiritual state. Fox did not support anarchism, the rejection of all civil authority and coercive power; rather, he supported judicious, compassionate use of coercive power to protect the innocent and to restrain wrongdoing.

- **Still, the Peace Testimony calls us always to open to others with a spirit of understanding, forgiveness, and reconciliation—"to see what love can do."**

- **I cannot do this by myself.** Living the Peace Testimony requires that I live from its Source: that I stand in the Light, see the truth of what I am, and yield to the Divine presence. Only then may I hope to "live in the virtue of that life and power that takes away the occasion of all war."

Some apparently come to God in a single, overwhelming moment. For others like myself, the process of submitting to the Light and becoming more faithful to Truth is slow and incremental, marked by small moments of opening and insight, then darkness and confusion, followed by rededication to regeneration and holiness. Each step of healing in the Spirit brings increased blessings of forgiveness, openness, and compassion. I am softened and emboldened, humbled and exalted, sobered and gladdened.

Reflecting back over the years, I send good will to Slug Malone, wherever he is—and to all whom I may have harmed in my failures to open more fully to the Light. Facing a frightening world of strife, bloodshed, and injustice, I rededicate myself to living peace—the royal law of love.

CHAPTER FIVE

HEALING GENDER HURT

Becoming A Quaker Man

With the dawning of my self-awareness as a boy comes the recognition that my sexual identity makes a profound difference. I differ from my three sisters, my mother, my maiden aunt, and my grandmother, who create the prevailing culture within my childhood home. The differences I note—rooted in my body and the role I am expected to fill—are those of power, labor, and degree of isolation.

I know that men rule the world. Monarchs, presidents, members of Congress, industrialists, financiers, and prominent figures of public life are nearly all male. In my own home, my Quaker father makes the final decision in major matters. The work of men seems both transcendently important and more laborious. Women's work is supportive, connective, sustaining the fabric of home and community; my father, with help from me and other males, produces the bulk of our economic well-being. As the females work close to the house with an endless round of tasks—washing dishes and clothes, cleaning house, canning vegetables, sewing, caring for chickens, gardening—I trudge to the barn or field to manhandle bales of hay, bushels of corn, farm machinery, and acres of mud and manure.

In winter the contrast grows stark: the warm, bright interior of the farmhouse is an island of comfort and cheer amid the frozen farmstead. Within the house is a constant chatter of activity, floods of words serving as the fluid of commerce. Outside on the land I move silently behind my taciturn father, or more often work by myself, engaging in some repetitive task—lifting bales of hay, shoveling manure, driving a tractor, building fences, hoeing weeds, managing hogs and cattle—alone with my thoughts. Summertime brings haying crews: jocular, worn men whose friendly banter, callused hands and hard sweat labor are worlds apart from the soft intimacy and bustling activity of the feminine world within the farmhouse. Some of the men bear wounds from their labor—missing fingers, portions of hands or even whole forearms, from unwisely trying to clear jams of cornstalks from a still-running harvester or silage chopper. Their bent frames remind me of a line from "The Man With A Hoe" by Edwin Markham: "Time's tragedy is in that aching stoop."[1] The men do not mention their infirmities, which are shouldered without complaint.

At school I learn of other differences. Forbidden to fight, I spend recess time either warding off blows or hiding in humiliation with younger children, pretending that I am doing as I wish. I inhabit a more physically dangerous world than my sisters: for them, safety and well-being come from being with others, while

I find safety only in solitude. Alone I find respite from violence and can reflect upon what I share in common with my fellow human beings.[2] My traumas of disrespect and abuse, rejection and exclusion instill in me a lifetime of reflexive anguish on behalf of others who suffer.

Fleeing from physical abuse has left me with doubts about my courage. Can I face up to threat, or has Quakerism made me into a coward? In my early 20's I resolve to test my bravery: I will challenge my fear of heights by jumping out of an airplane. In Orange, Massachusetts, I train for three hours in sport parachuting, then clamber (with a main parachute on my back and a reserve chute on my chest) into a plane along with some eight other equally frightened jumpers. One-half mile above the earth, my time has come. I edge toward an opening in the fuselage. When tapped by the instructor, I launch myself blindly into the empty air, with nothing between me and the earth below. At that instant something strikes me on the forehead. I have no clue what it is. Then the static line yanks my ripcord, the chute deploys—and I feel an overwhelming rush of relief and joy: "I'm not going to die!" Drifting gently downward in the breeze, I am in heaven.

After landing and disentangling myself from the parachute, I realize that what had struck me on the forehead was my own hand, caught by the 100-miles-per-hour gale that swept by the plane in flight. I was too lost in panic to recognize what was happening. In coming weeks I return for three more jumps, until I am finally satisfied: when I judge it to be necessary, I can do what terrifies me. My reassurance is sweet—I have laid a demon to rest.

Quakerism holds up ideals of manhood that are strikingly at odds with conventional gender norms. Whereas traditional masculinity calls for hardening one's emotional body and readiness to impose one's will upon others, Quakerism promotes gentleness and nonviolence. Quakerism values equality and mutuality over the hierarchies of authority and subordination (typically enforced by males) that are entrenched in public culture. Competition is the rule in the public economic order, whereas Quakerism favors cooperation and mutual support.

By no means do Quaker men always embody these "nonmasculine" virtues. It is impossible to grow up in our culture without absorbing some of its biases—and Quakers are as prone as others to moral failure. Competing expectations create for Quaker men more than the usual confusion about gender identity. Conflicts between men and women—the so-called "war of the sexes"—are probably as common among Friends as non-Friends. Thus the task before us is to unite the two great Quaker testimonies of equality and peace.

Where I Stand

To this work I bring no special wisdom. I hope only to be myself, engaging in honest dialogue with others, trusting that as we yield to service from the deepest integrity we can discern, all may see more clearly—and find our way to a healing of the heart. I write not as a disembodied mind, pretending impartial objectivity. Rather, I write as a man of European descent, having been granted through no choice of my own—simply on the basis of my gender and color—privileges of which I am only partially aware. I write as a thoroughly sexual being embodied in a male body, with its own unique history, formed in a particular time and place, writing from my singular perspective. I write as a philosopher with a spiritual and psychological bent, seeking to comprehend my life in its broadest context.

I write also as a casualty in the war of the sexes. From females I have sustained my deepest and most lingering emotional wounds, incurred through mutual ignorance, envy, mistrust, and cruelty. With females, I have felt shamed, humiliated, silenced, undervalued, cut to the quick. I have vented my hurt and anger at women in ways more wounding than I will ever know. With women, I have also felt my deepest joys.

I write also as a victim in my youth of violence and sexual abuse by other males.

And I write as a Friend, shaped from childhood by Quaker faith and practice, awed by Quaker spirituality, at odds with (and often in denial of) my impulses toward violence, abhorring the violence of others, and committed to healing. I look to Quakerism for resources in healing gender hurt. As a Friend, I aspire to speak from personal experience, from what I know "experimentally." Though subtle, the truth about gender healing is not remote, but close at hand, hidden only by our own blindness. We know it in our bones and can find it exemplified in lives we see—and indeed, in our own lives.

Academic Adventures

When I quit drinking, I resolved that I would never again divorce my professional and personal lives. Healing gender hurt became a top personal priority—in my own life, and in the lives of others. I was proud of the Quaker history of relative gender equality and the courageous Quaker feminists of the past 200 years. A Women's Studies colleague urged me to teach a course in the philosophy of feminism. With the blessing of members of my department, I began teaching a course, "Human Liberation," with these objectives:

- To promote a deeper understanding of the root notion of freedom;
- To become more aware of our own gender conditioning

and the gender conditioning of persons of the other sex;

- To explore the consequences of gender roles for women and men, and to recognize where they are oppressive;

- To liberate ourselves from attitudes and behaviors that oppress us and others;

- To enrich our lives together as women and men: to facilitate understanding and mutual support, to enlarge our options in relationships—between men and men, women and women, and women and men—and to heal the wounds of the "war of the sexes."

My students read philosophical analyses of freedom, followed by writings on women's liberation and the new men's movement.[3] I attended pro-feminist men's conferences and retreats, always with the agenda of both deepening my grasp of academic findings, and promoting gender healing for my students and myself. With a sociologist and a political scientist, I created a new Men's Studies course, "Men and Masculinity."[4] Women flooded the course; men were somewhat more cautious recruits. In addition to assigning scholarly materials, I employed classroom exercises to heighten our awareness of gender conditioning and promote mutual insight. Gender role reversal games were potent learning tools, generating much laughter and some genuine learning. Because of the high profile of the women's movement, men who entered the course already anticipated some of what they would encounter. In contrast, realizing the costs of masculinity for men themselves was a difficult lesson for those whose worldview allowed for only women to be seen as victims of gender hurt, and men to be only perpetrators and beneficiaries.

My courses include exploration of issues of homosexuality, homophobia, and heterosexism. A nationally-known and rabidly homophobic neoconservative political scientist at my college attacks me publicly, stuffing all faculty mailboxes with a scurrilous piece

entitled, "Sodomy and the Academy." He privately sug-
gests to others that I am probably homosexual. He
challenges me to a public debate; I decline, but invite
him to speak to my class. My departmental colleagues
march into my office to declare that if I will not en-
gage in public battle with him, they will take up my de-
fense. They do so—and he challenges the entire depart-
ment to a public debate on the topic, "Resolved: That
Homosexuality Is an Unnatural Vice." (He is to argue
the affirmative, they the negative, with the President
of the college to preside, and the Dean of the Faculty
to be the timekeeper.) My colleagues decline this pre-
posterous proposal, and I finally write a public reply
to him, refuting his arguments while striking a concil-
iatory tone.

Forms of Power

In addition to its evident benefits for students, my immersion in gender studies gave me a richer understanding of my own
gender identity. I share some of this learning here:

Blinded by the dominant culture, as a boy I had associated
power exclusively with the public realm, entailing hierarchies
of authority, control of economic goods, exercise of police and
military force, and ultimately the threat of destruction. Public
power was the coin of masculine dominance, exercised often
for ill. I did not reflect on alternate modes of power: power as
efficacy, power as vitality and joyful connectedness, and power
in aesthetic, emotional, and spiritual dimensions. As feminist
writers observe, power is more than simply "power over," that
is, the ability to coerce others to act as one wishes. Bertrand
Russell defined power in the broadest sense as "the production of intended effects,"[5] including any ability to bring about a
perceived good. Thus a relatively powerful person is one who

usually can achieve what he or she chooses, whereas a powerless person lacks such ability. Drawing upon Quaker economist
Kenneth Boulding's *Three Faces of Power*,[6] I distinguish between
integrative power and *threat power*. Integrative power is the
ability to bring about desired results through affection, giving,
loyalty, caring, and other forms of bonding. A person who is able
to create and maintain strong friendships has a significant form
of integrative power, for example. The greatest of human goods,
including self-esteem, appreciation of beauty, and love itself, are
expressions of effective integrative power.

Threat power, the ability to control others through instill-
ing fear of unpleasant consequences, is used to secure goods
produced by other means. Threat power includes much more
than blatant intimidation; for example, common forms of
threat power are simple expressions of disapproval. Frowns,
ridicule, coldness, ostracism, and other such displays are pervasive means by which societal norms are enforced; we conform
because we fear rejection and exclusion. In particular, anger is
often intended (and experienced by others) as a threat, suggest-
ing possible withdrawal of love, limitations of freedom, or other
forms of punishment or retaliation. When we get angry at others,
we are employing one of the most common forms of threat
power.

To control their children, most parents use a variety of
explicit and implied threats of unpleasant consequences, from
simple disapproval to loss of privileges to corporeal punishment.
In the workplace, motivation to perform well typically includes
fear of the consequences of failure, and in supervising others,
we are likely to use not only "carrots" but also "sticks." Reliance
upon threat power is found in any group or institution that exercises authority over potentially resisting others. The law itself is a
massive and complex instrument of threat power, ideally rationalized by justice and fairness. We legislate penalties for murder,
theft, rape, molestation, and so on to deter unwanted behavior

and to establish guidelines for an acceptable social environment. Legalized threat power is deemed necessary in virtually every society to protect, maintain, and enhance valuable social bonds and economic goods. (Not all uses of legalized threat power are benign, of course; the mechanism of law may enforce exploitation and bolster unjust privilege.) Closely allied with legal sanctions are moral sanctions. Moral disapproval is generally experienced as unpleasant and may indicate readiness to deter or punish the unwanted behavior. When we judge another to be morally lacking, we are usually exercising threat power.

Gendered Power

Women and men in all societies exercise both integrative and threat power. In most societies, however, males assume a larger role in the use of threat power (particularly its harsher forms) and females are assigned a larger role in the use of integrative power. In his wide-ranging review of manhood as an achieved status in cultures around the world, *Manhood in the Making: Cultural Concepts of Masculinity*, anthropologist David Gilmore identifies certain "nearly universal features which may be regarded as training for the exercise of threat power."[7] In society after society, from aboriginal people of Oceania, South America, and East Africa to traditional cultures of the Mediterranean, China, India, Japan, to modern North America, Gilmore discovers a culturally-sanctioned emphasis for males on toughness, aggressiveness, bravery, and stoicism in the face of danger and pain, exacted at great physical and emotional cost to the males who are made to undergo it. Gilmore calls this pattern "stressed masculinity," to reflect both the cultural pressures upon males to exhibit it, as well as its psychic and physical costs to males themselves. I learned that my experiences on the playgrounds of my elementary school were but one small instance of a world-wide pattern of harsh induction into a male role.

If stressed masculinity is a cultural artifact rather than a bio-logical necessity (as Gilmore believes), why is it virtually univer-sal? Gilmore notes that "Those cultures that have a pronounced manhood ideology seem to be the ones that have chosen fight as a survival strategy. Without a genetic imprinting, men in those cultures have to be conditioned to be brave in order to fight."[8] This analysis is reinforced by Gilmore's examination of two ex-ceptions to the pattern: Tahiti and Semai. Both cultures have largely rejected fighting and belligerence, and not coinciden-tally display a high degree of sexual indeterminacy or androg-yny. Gilmore writes that Tahitian men "are no more aggressive than women; women do not seem 'softer' or more 'maternal' than men... . (M)en and women also have roles so similar as to seem almost indistinguishable... . (T)here is no stress on proving manhood, no pressure on men to appear in any significant way different from women or children."[9] "Men share a cultural value of 'timidity' which forbids retaliation, and even when provoked men rarely come to blows."[10] Perhaps Tahitian men are rela-tively peaceful partly because living is easy in their lush tropical climate; Gilmore notes that "The harsher the environment and the scarcer the resources, the more manhood is stressed as in-spiration and goal."[11] Perhaps also the island isolation of Tahitian society provides natural insulation from marauding outsiders, so that fighting in defense of one's resources seems less necessary.

The second exception noted by Gilmore, the Semai of central Malaysia, are able to avoid most conflict with others simply by running away. Abhorring violence and conflict, the Semai have adopted a survival strategy of "fleeing rather than fighting."[12] Gilmore reports that Western observers invariably describe the Semais as "weak" and "timid": "Whenever trouble arises, they either immediately capitulate, or else they disappear in the forest."[13]

The Hollowness of Threat Power

In summary, Gilmore observes that "when men are conditioned to fight, manhood is important; where men are conditioned to flight, the opposite. Just why most societies have chosen fight... probably is related to the general scarcity of resources and the inability of most societies to run away, like the Semai, into open wilderness."[14] He continues:

> Because of the universal urge to flee from danger, we may regard "real" manhood as an inducement for high performance in the social struggle for scarce resources, a code of conduct that advances collective interests by overcoming inner inhibitions. In fulfilling their obligations, men stand to lose—a hovering threat that separates them from women and boys. They stand to lose their reputations or their lives; yet their prescribed tasks must be done if the group is to survive and prosper. Because boys must steel themselves to enter into such struggles, they must be prepared by various sorts of tempering and toughening. To be men, most of all, they must accept the fact that they are expendable. This acceptance of expendability constitutes the basis of the manly pose wherever it is encountered.[15]

Thus the primary social function of stressed masculinity is the exercise of threat power to serve and protect the in-group. In most societies, this task has fallen primarily upon males, perhaps because of their greater average size and physical strength, and because they are less needed for gestation, birthing, and nurturing children. (Women can be fully as fierce as men, of course—especially in the direct defense of their loved ones.)

Requiring self-denial, risk, and pain, stressed masculinity does not come easily. Males must be initiated into their socially prescribed roles, usually by other males. For better or worse, the subjection of boys to stressed masculinity continues in our own culture—through athletic activities, ridicule of softness, laziness and cowardice, and a conditional love that bestows approval only when demanding expectations are met.

Because it denies fear, stressed masculinity promotes exaggerated levels of anger. Much if not all of male anger is masked fear. Because it views men as expendable, stressed masculinity also invites denial of death itself: hence the exuberant and often foolhardy risk-taking of many young men in our culture, in a pattern of self-destructiveness that one author has dubbed "macho-psychotic."[16]

Stressed masculinity separates thought from feeling and destroys healthy self-care with a body-denying ideology—thus accounting for much of the disparity between men and women in longevity, health, and psychological well-being. The exercise of integrative power tends to enhance life and health, for self and others: we flourish more readily under conditions of love, trust, connectedness, and affiliation with nurturing others. In contrast, the exercise of threat power tends to be life- and health-diminishing, for self and others. In mounting a threat—whether of simple anger, or a harsher sanction of some kind—I must steel myself against unpleasant reactions, closing off to empathy for others and to my own fear and need. Threat power is the essence of objectification: when I exercise threat power, the other becomes less a person, a center of self-governing will, and more an object or thing to be manipulated and controlled. When I employ threat power I must shut down a part of myself, objectifying my own body and feelings. Threat power separates and alienates, promoting a fortress mentality of lonely autonomy and the expectation of self-sufficiency. If exercise of threat power becomes second nature over a lifetime of meeting stringent social expectations, the implications for longevity and health are not difficult to discern.

Our culture tends to identify power exclusively with control based upon implied threat. In our own and most other cultures, such power is overwhelmingly in the hands of males. If power is exclusively threat power, men are indeed the more powerful sex. But power includes the ability to bring about *any* perceived good, including meeting one's own basic needs—and in this regard, men are often relatively powerless. Trained to exercise threat power, often themselves targets of threat power—at work and play, in public and private—men become sadly deficient in integrative power and consequently handicapped in taking care of themselves. Men thus become dependent upon women to meet basic human needs, while (in the service of threat power) denying their very dependency.[17]

So long as any good is scarce—food, water, comfortable and attractive living space, and so on—and so long as humans themselves fall short of complete altruism, it would appear that conflict can be averted only through an uneasy balance of competing threats, and some persons will need to be trained in the effective exercise of threat power. In this view, threat power is a necessary evil, unavoidable but costly, both to those over whom it is exercised and to those who exercise it. As noted in the previous chapter, early Friends did not insist upon a total rejection of all threat power, regardless of circumstances. In order to respond to threat with nonviolence and loving-kindness, we must (as Gandhi observed) undergo demanding training and spiritual discipline.

To admit that we need some threat power is not to justify its use in every situation, however. Much avoidable human suffering arises from gratuitous and excessive use of threat power. Because men are assigned a larger role in the exercise of threat power, they are also its greatest abusers; for example, male prisoners outnumber female prisoners by a ratio of about eighteen to one.[18] The abuse of threat power by men has been called "toxic masculinity"[19]: swaggering macho belligerence, rape and sexual abuse, destruction of the natural environment, and a host of other evils. As Abraham Maslow once observed, if the only tool you have is a hammer, then everything begins to look like a nail. Reliance upon threat is a tacit admission of failure and weakness; we must learn to recognize it as such. Instead of being taught to admire toughness, dominance, repression of empathy, and extreme competitiveness, we must learn to recognize the cost of such behaviors and to avoid them as much as possible. Greater involvement of fathers in parenting; more training in nonviolent conflict resolution at every level; reduction of television, video, and other media violence—these and many other steps may help to curb toxic masculinity and to reduce the exercise of threat power to that essential minimum required for discipline and order within the home and workplace, and on the streets and abroad.[20]

Foundations of Gender Justice

Stressed masculinity must be purged of its toxic elements. We know that this is possible—men who are courageous, strong and sensitive, able both to protect and nurture loved ones, possessing the ability to establish clear boundaries and stand by them. In a dangerous world we need good boundaries to manage our fear, both to ward off danger and to create a safe haven or home within which fear may be reduced, making space for the freer exercise of integrative power.

With these concessions to an imperfect world, I return to my primary commitment. Complicit at a thousand levels with a society framed by the exercise of threat power, and unable honestly to affirm absolute pacifism, I nevertheless claim nonviolence as my path and goal. As we share the burden of threat, I invite my sisters and brothers to work together on our essential moral task: to replace threat power with integrative power and fear with love, without endangering fundamental goods of life, healthy, safety, compassion, and human flourishing. Viewed not as an absolute, unbending doctrine but as a working hypothesis inspired by faith, commitment to nonviolence may help us to realize more fully an ideal exalted in our various religious traditions: the primacy of love.

As in other efforts at reconciliation, peace must be built upon genuine justice. Women's oppression—the various "glass ceilings" that limit their advancement in political, economic, and religious roles, their relative economic deprivation and poverty, their victimization by violent men, the appalling facts of sexual abuse, their disproportionate burdens in child care, the entrenched male bias in virtually all realms of public discourse, and much more—these things must be constructively addressed before one can speak with integrity of peace and harmony between the sexes. John Calvi, a Friend who has devoted his own life to the healing of trauma, declares,

> In every group of people from every continent I have worked with, (the) burden of sexual hurt is frequently an additional part of the women's history. Perhaps it is so commonplace throughout human time, (that) we do not see it as clearly apart and distinct from plague, famine, refugees fleeing war, or war itself.

> The sense that this common thread weaves together women's lives around the globe is almost too much to take in. Yet as I connect the dots of what I have seen and heard, I know that it is so. And I grieve this. The reality of sexual hurt is a horrible burden. As someone who's survived rape as a young child, I know too well the nature of the pain and the tremendous work that this healing entails. The list of damages is long and ugly: diminished self-worth, physical illnesses, trust broken nearly beyond repair, and flaming swirls of anger, fear, guilt, and sadness. And if truly safe places are few and far between, where and when can healing begin?[21]

The work of gender justice is too often assumed to be a matter of grudging male concessions to self-righteous female critics. Such a misconception obscures men's own deep wounding by pressures to conform to societal expectations of their own gender role. To Calvi's horrifying litany of women's gender hurt, we must add the unimaginable toll for men of war-related deaths and maiming (both physical and emotional), as well as the traditional costs of the male role, in decreased longevity, stress-related disease, higher rates of successful suicide attempts, reduced capacity for intimacy and affiliation, burdens of assuming an active and responsible role, and other "hazards of being male." These also must be acknowledged and addressed if peacemaking efforts can hope to be effective.[22] Quaker activism at its best is not partisan empowerment (one group gaining at the expense of another), but a mutual, inclusive empowerment.

The Joy of Gender Healing

Central to Quaker belief and practice from the beginning has been the insight that opposition and strife arise from separation from the Spirit, and that in opening fully to our own depths, we open to our unity with one another. Once we have come to experience the oneness of all persons in Spirit, we can no longer define others simply as enemies to be overcome. We must instead regard them as precious and sacred in their own right, and at the deepest level in harmony with ourselves. Effective social change comes not from outwitting or suppressing resistance, but rather of appealing to that of God in every person. Such an appeal requires that we relinquish our own egocentric agendas and submit to our Inward Teacher.

The beginning of this work is listening: not a partial listening of one who is already formulating a rejoinder, but—in the spirit of Quaker worship—listening with an open heart and mind, so that space opens for each person to speak with his or her own true voice. I do not ask that women cease to call attention to their oppression and suffering, nor do I ask of myself and other men that we remain silent regarding our own suffering. Each should be heard and responded to. Neither should be used to discount the other; nor is it fruitful to argue which is greater, more damaging, more unfair or unjust. What is needed is a framework of understanding within which each suffering voice may be heard and each damaged life taken into healing. We need to enlarge our circle of compassion, to hear one another's pain, to step out of the cycle of recrimination, defensiveness, and counterattack.

As we do this, we may find that our pain is a source of wisdom. In our wounds lies our strength, and the measures of our travail are simultaneously indices of hope. Through inwardness opened by effort and suffering, we may come to know our unity with other beings. Such opening is the way of true communion. Discerning the Sacred within another, we humble ourselves before it, acknowledging our imperfections as our own. From this moral vision we are emboldened to address injustice by a sharing in the Spirit.

At its best, Quaker service is joyful subversion, making common cause with all of creation. No longer a grim and earnest affair, revolution becomes celebration, an act of play. The luminosity of creation shines forth, inspiring moral action. From such a vantage point, it becomes impossible to point an accusing finger of blame. The gifts of each are before our eyes, the magnificent contributions of women and men alike—always present to our eyes, if we are but willing to see.

Quaker peacemaking in the war of the sexes thus manifests clarity of purpose—for example, by witnessing against sexist stereotyping, spousal abuse, or economic injustice—while reaching out to those engaged in wrongdoing. Abandoning self-righteousness, it recognizes that all of us are complicit in varying degrees in maintaining a cultural system that causes gender hurt. Genuine healing of that hurt comes through awakening to and acting from our underlying unity in the Spirit, for which no individual may take credit.

For myself and my brothers, I carry this hope: that we may open ourselves to the pervasive, often brutal realities of women's oppression and take steps to correct it. When women rage against us; when they insist upon their prerogatives at seemingly the most inopportune times; when they draw back in hostility because of centuries of injustice and abuse still repeated today; when their awareness of their suffering is at last too much, producing a revolt of the flesh, may we beware of asking that they be more compassionate and forgiving, remembering that women have traditionally been expected to be empathetic and compassionate. Men's call for compassion may disguise an expectation that women overlook their own oppression and remain subordinate. Instead, may we men become more compassionate.

May we realize that beneath women's fury may be deeper hurt: desperation that they cannot love us as they want to love, a sadness at their separation from us. For as we need to love them, we know that they need to love us.

For my sisters, I carry this hope: when we men draw back from your protests, no matter how gently couched; when we seem indifferent or defensive, or are unwilling to listen; when we go about our lives as if your concerns were trivial, seemingly secure in our privilege, I invite you to reflect that within us is also buried pain, suppressed by a cultural imperative that imposes great costs upon males who admit to weakness and dependency upon others—an imperative that drives us away from our inwardness toward outward performance. What looks like male power to women may feel like a heavy burden of responsibility and demand to men. Our numbness hastens us to our graves, alienating us from ourselves and from you—most of all, from our deep need to love. For as you need to love us, we also need to love you.

For all, I carry this hope: that we learn to care through our pain; that we find within ourselves the courage to yield tremulously to the possibility of intimacy and the promise of love. As we explore the darker, fearful reaches of ourselves, trusting the Sacred Ground of our unity with one another, may we discover an easing of hardness, a softening of edges, an opening into playfulness and the possibility of love. As beauty insinuates into ideology, stealing away our sharpness before we are aware, may we emerge from an anxious flatness into an infinitely yielding, immeasurable depth.

May we see and hear one another as never before—and thereby know ourselves for the first time. Men loving women loving men loving women, women loving women, men loving men: healing gender hurt calls us to our deepest selves, inviting us to approach one another with acts of reconciliation, of mutual healing and love, sharing together the work of justice in a spirit of joy.

CHAPTER SIX

FRIENDLY PEDAGOGY

Spiritual Roots

My father sits alone on the top facing bench, his gaunt frame hunched over the tiny clerk's table, presiding over our Quarterly Meeting for Worship on the Occasion of Business. The plain wooden benches in the century-old building are filled with sober, expectant Friends, gathered to participate in this exercise in corporate discernment. An air of solemnity pervades the room. My father's elevation is misleading; he does not sit higher than others in order to lead and direct, but rather to listen, observe, and sense the movement of the Spirit—something we are all called to do. The clerk is expected to be well-informed about the business before the Meeting; to draft an agenda; to share necessary information with those assembled; to pose questions for all to consider; to discern "the sense of the meeting" as it emerges and give voice to that sense; and to draft minutes that accurately reflect our corporate discernment.

My father introduces a matter that requires the Meeting's attention. After some initial discussion, a weighty Friend rises to propose a possible resolution. Her words are followed by a period of worshipful silence as Friends reflect. Another expresses concerns. More silence. Yet another Friend suggests how the ideas of the first speaker might be modified to accommodate the reservations just expressed. A barely audible murmur of assent ripples through the room. After a suitable wait, my father gives voice to that assent— first orally, then in written form. His proposed minute is tested in the body of the Meeting. Finding that the wording meets with no objections (those who have doubts being willing to "stand aside"), he asks whether the Meeting is ready to affirm the minute. A chorus rises from the floor: "Approve!" We move on to the next item on the agenda.

The above scenario illustrates a successful instance of Friends' Meeting for Worship on the Occasion of Business, which "is guided by three core beliefs: that there is that of God in everyone, that each can experience that of God within, and that divine guidance will lead to the realization of a single shared truth."[1] Friends' distinctive manner of conducting business impressed me at an early age as a model for how persons of good will may cooperate in the search for truth. Growing into adulthood, I frequently found myself in non-Quaker settings where decisions were made by different procedures—aggressive advocacy by strong personalities who overrode softer voices; rhetoric intended to sway the emotions rather than appeal to settled insight; votes pushed through over objections of a disgruntled minority; and the elaborate intricacies of Roberts Rules of Order.

Even as I resigned myself to navigating these choppy waters, I yearned for the gentle, loving decision procedures that I had experienced as a child.

When I finally earned my graduate degree and was given responsibility for my own classrooms, I was allowed to structure them according to my best judgment. My teaching instincts were then given freer reign. In the early years of my teaching career, however, I did not realize how deeply those instincts were rooted in my Quaker experience. Only years later did I see that the deliberate and respectful procedures of Quaker process undergirded my approach.[2]

I focus here upon affinities between clerking a fruitful Meeting for Business and the underlying themes of Quaker pedagogy. There is much in Quaker process that is out of place in a secular college classroom, of course. In such a classroom, one may not presume a shared religious purpose or indeed, any spiritual values. Unlike Friends' Meeting for Business, a classroom is rarely a venue for corporate decision-making. Teachers are typically viewed as authority figures who direct and evaluate the performances of a cohort of learners—a hierarchical model that is at odds with good Quaker process. No sensible clerk assigns papers or problem sets, administers examinations, and grades the resulting work. In view of these differences, how can we draw upon one to inform the other?

Yet the contrasts cloak deeper affinities between good Quaker process and fruitful pedagogy. If (as Friends believe) there is no final division between the sacred and the secular, there is also no place where one must abandon Friends' faith and practice in order to teach well. Quaker spirituality features deep listening to the inklings of truth within oneself and others.[3] All are presumed to have personal, direct access to some aspects of this truth. Skills of discernment vary from person to person, and some have acquired more information than others regarding any particular issue. Yet good Quaker process is founded upon a deep respect for all who are present, and a readiness to honor the insights that each may bring.

These affinities account for much of the attractiveness of Quaker educational ideals. In exploring them here, I draw upon the work of numerous scholars who have developed a rich account of Quaker schools and the educational perspectives that they foster.[4] The pedagogical questions that I hope to clarify include these:

- Where is the authority of knowledge to be found?
- What is the connection between classroom learning and the rest of life?
- If, indeed, there is that of God in everyone, what does this realization mean for the relationship of teacher and student?
- If all are endowed with a measure of the Light and no one can claim authority over the inner life of another, what does this mean for the traditional hierarchies of pedagogical authority and power?
- If, as Friends' spiritual heritage implies, we may regain the harmony between humans and the creation that was lost in Adam's fall, what are the implications for empirical study of the natural world?

The Priority of Experience

A spirituality that locates authority and truth within each person rather than some external voice naturally lends itself to a pedagogy that does the same. The role of the teacher is not to deposit knowledge into the learner from whence it may be withdrawn[5]; although the teacher offers information to invite insight, true learning occurs only when students themselves awaken to that insight and make it their own. Those charged with instructing others may not somehow stuff that learning into the craws of their students and expect it to be retained in proper form.

Teaching and learning in Quaker perspective are prefigured by the Platonic view that all true knowledge is gained through re-directing one's attention. As Socrates asserts, "Education isn't what some people declare it to be, putting knowledge into souls that lack it, like putting sight into blind eyes... (but rather) the power to learn is present in everyone's soul... education takes for granted that sight is there but that it isn't turned the right way or looking where it ought to look, and it tries to redirect it appropriately."[6]

Sight is already in the soul—but our inward eye turns away from truth. Redirecting that inward vision means awakening more fully to our own experience and seeing into its meaning. Thus instruction or education requires skillful questioning that invites us down a path of insight, not simply to a destination pre-ordained by the questioner, but to a deeper intimacy with ex-perienced reality itself. Education is liberation, an open-ended process in which we grow larger, see more, and open more fully to the world.

Inspired by Friends' spirituality, Parker Palmer writes, "Only as doctrine has experiential validity can it be honored at all. The important question is not what the text says, but what it says that can be validated by you. Whether the subject is literature or atomic physics, the test is always experiential (or experimen-tal)."[7] When the nominal subject of learning is a seemingly inert piece of data—a mathematical formula, a biological finding, a political trend—still, the central moment of teaching and learning is not a mechanical transfer of that information from one data bank to another, but a personal, intimate realization of truth, when the light of consciousness flares and expands in insight, and one can say, "Oh! I see!" Michael D. Smith, Dean of the Harvard Faculty of Arts and Sciences, puts the point simply: "One of the most important goals of a liberal arts education today is to give students the personal experience of discovery."[8]

To cultivate such moments of enlightenment, teacher and

learner must have faith that they are indeed possible—by (in Thoreau's resonant phrase) "an infinite expectation of the dawn." When learners who have lost this hope come to see education as joyless and irrelevant—perhaps through too many experiences of failure, or through harshly coercive prodding—it may still be possible for miracles to occur, when they encounter an instructor who believes in their potential for insight, growth, and productivity.

Many years ago I gained from an unexpected source an appreciation of what fosters such miracles:

Presence in the Classroom

Following the end of my first marriage, I am dating a woman who makes her living as a professional actress. I take her on a walking tour of my college campus, showing her a classroom where I had once been delivering a lecture on Immanuel Kant to some 30 students when a stray dog trotted through the open classroom door and up the aisle. Instantly, all attention in the room shifted from my words to the dog. I had totally lost my audience. Knowing that I could not compete, I paused, and the dog passed through the maze of desk chairs and exited. Making a lame joke, I resumed my lecture.

When she hears my story, the actress retorts, "Oh yes—the dog has much more presence than you do!" At first taken aback, I realize that she does not intend to insult me. A stray animal or a baby are scene stealers of the first order; their unselfconscious, natural presence breaks the spell woven by any actress, actor—or teacher.

This realization leads me to an intriguing question: if I learn to enter wholly and unselfconsciously into

my classroom encounters with students, might I have
as much presence for them as did the dog?

Arresting experiences of presence occur in many settings. In the course of a Friends' Meeting for Business, it sometimes happens that everyone in the room senses power and unity. Such moments inspire gladness and awe. At such a moment, a wandering pet would be unlikely to break the spell and might even be experienced as a part of the wonder.

In my own teaching experience, I have seen inspiration occasionally approach such heights. They were not, however, when I was shining as a performing star; in fact, they were more likely to occur when I had been momentarily forgotten by my students, as they awakened to insights that engaged their whole being—often when they were interacting with others in the classroom. I was privileged to suspend my professorial role and simply witness what unfolded before me.

Although a sensitive teacher may foster opportunities for such moments, classroom presence cannot be manufactured by clever pedagogical technique. It is a gift of grace, as space opens for teaching and learning to meld into unity, inviting our surrender to insight. At such times, good pedagogy reveals itself to be a form of spiritual practice.

Integrity

Friends' insistence upon lived experience as the fount of true knowledge fosters an uncommon commitment to moral consistency: to live daily in accord with an experiential conviction of truth. The classroom is continuous with the whole of life, and the exercise of our intellects must be situated within the natural environment of our bodily identities, social relationships, and spiritual orientation.

The pedagogical implications of integrity are many and profound. Responsible teaching and learning require rigorous self-examination: can my claim be validated by what I actually experience? Such care in observation is an essential feature of sound scientific method, and of the thoughtful study of a literary text, a logical proof, an historical document.

More broadly: what goes on in an educational institution should not be divorced from what goes on outside. George Fox challenged his fellow Quakers to "Let your lives speak"—and in fact, our lives *do* speak, often more loudly than our words. Responsible pedagogy connects academic matters with the rest of life—by bringing a class in ecology to the bank of a polluted river, by noting the barrio a few blocks away from a classroom discussion of immigration policy, or otherwise drawing upon actual, concrete examples from the experience of students to make learning come alive.

When we engage in academic discourse not rooted in the anchor of our personal experience, our minds are severed from our bodies, our ideas from our actions. Flights of abstract fantasy leave behind the concrete circumstances of our lives. Whatever its appeal, such language invites hypocrisy. Words and symbols are themselves forms of behavior: when we seek genuine insight, what we say should be both appropriate and sound. Truth is not merely something that we know, but also something that we do.

The Facts Are Friendly

If Quaker pedagogy invites us into engagement with the world, it also sees that world as approachable and ultimately welcoming. The conception of the natural world as ineluctably "fallen" and shot through with sin—a view attributed to the Genesis account of Adam and Eve's transgression and God's resulting punishment, and elaborated at great length in Calvinist theology—entails a spirituality at odds with the world it surveys. While early Friends certainly were burdened by the sinfulness of their own and others' lives, they also (as shown in Fox's central mystical opening) believed that we may recover in our lifetime the original harmony between God and humans. Quaker scholar Melvin Keiser observes, "Beneath our sinful experience of a distorted world is the illumined experience of the world in its original freshness and power permeated by divine presence."[9] God speaks to us everywhere, calling us to revere and restore the natural order.

Awakening to a "new creation," Friends saw that our original unity with the natural world may be rediscovered and enjoyed, allowed them to enter into scientific studies with a sense of welcoming trust. A respectful empirical observation of the world reveals God's presence, wrote William Penn:

It were happy if we studied nature more in natural things, and acted according to nature, whose rules are few, plain, and most reasonable... . The heavens, earth, and waters... would be better understood by us; and an eternal wisdom, power, majesty, and goodness very conspicuous to us through those sensible and passing forms, the world wearing the mark of its Maker, Whose stamp is everywhere visible and the characters very legible to the children of wisdom.[10]

Reflecting a "nature-friendly" theology, Friends in the 18th and 19th centuries were well represented among the ranks of scientific thinkers and within The Royal Society. In the early years of the American colonies, a number of prominent naturalists were Quakers.

Invite All Voices

The radical egalitarianism of early Friends challenged authoritarian hierarchies of all kinds. In the face of efforts to silence and exclude them, Friends broke through with prophetic power. As Jesus welcomed into his presence the outcasts, the rejected and despised, so early Friends transgressed the prevailing social order by a "disorderly" eruption of the Spirit. The Quaker testimony of equality is ideally not the assertion of a superficial unity achieved by silencing dissident voices, but rather a richer unity in diversity that seeks the fullest presence of all. Such a discovery of deeper unity can arise only when all voices are heard.

Thus Quaker pedagogy invites all voices into the dialogue, with the conviction that each may bring some measure of light and truth. To notice silent students and sense the meaning of their nonverbal behavior, to communicate appreciation for their presence, and if they gain courage to speak, to welcome their contributions—this respectful, expectant listening mirrors the process of Quaker worship itself. Likewise, Quaker pedagogy invites an awakening of our silenced internal voices, to move toward greater wholeness and an undivided self—thereby awakening to the power of the Spirit within.

If true education awakens, empowers, and liberates, then a teacher's role is to facilitate these processes. Traditional educational agendas have typically functioned to induct students into an approved ideology, thereby subordinating them to existing power structures. Quaker pedagogy is unsettling to such agendas, since it posits in each learner a sacredness and potential wisdom to which all should be answerable, seeking (in Nelle Morton's memorable phrase) to "hear human beings to speech,"[11]—that is, to liberate the unique narrative that constitutes the experiential insight of each person.

Friends' treasuring of that of God within every person and their insistence upon hearing every voice provide fertile ground for feminist thought. At a time when the very idea of female ministers was cause for ridicule, George Fox, Margaret Fell, and other early Friends insisted that the Spirit was accessible to women and men alike—and that anyone through whom the Spirit moves has a duty to respond, regardless of gender. Four of the five signers of the 1848 Seneca Falls Declaration of Women's

Rights were Friends; and many of the brightest luminaries of the 19th-century women's movement were likewise Friends—including Lucretia Mott, Susan B. Anthony, and Alice Paul, the author of the Equal Rights Amendment.[12]

Quaker-inspired feminism approaches issues of inclusiveness and gender equality with a straightforward, unapologetic assumption that *of course* equality should be reflected in our words, actions, and policies. Without grounding in the Spirit, the drive for equality too often degenerates into reaction, bitterness, and even violence—whereas a spiritual practice that diminishes fear also defuses reaction and polarization. The voice of social justice at its best is serene and unapologetic, ready to confront evil while remaining open to and accepting of the evil-doer. Thus the reality of God within not only confirms the fundamental worth of everyone, but also, through its life-giving reassurance of divine power and grace, reduces fear born of perceived weakness—thus enabling one to affirm equality without becoming rancorous or abusive.

What does such spiritually-based inclusiveness mean in a classroom? The root assumptions of equality and mutual respect properly set the tone. Those from groups that have historically been marginalized and silenced are assured of inclusion, while those from groups that have historically been privileged find that assumption no longer obtains, yet are themselves not demonized or shamed.

In actual practice, however, lingering trenchant legacies of racism, sexism, classism, and other forms of oppression distort every educational endeavor to some degree. Friends' spiritual experience does not inoculate against the eruption of these injustices—but at least provides a vision of equality, as well as the insight to claim and live into that vision.

How are these messages of inclusiveness and empowerment to be communicated without inviting a host of abuses? Put bluntly, how does a teacher make space for "hearing students into speech" without inviting garbage? A student-centered classroom can privilege the loudest voices; it can valorize a shallow relativism; it can undermine the natural authority of truth itself.

Clerking the Classroom

Patterns of Quaker spirituality are again helpful in addressing these real dangers. As manifested in a gathered Meeting for Worship, Friends value careful listening and encourage speaking from a deeply reflective place that respects all who are present. Underlying such attitudes is a reverence for truth itself as a reality that makes claims upon us all. As Parker Palmer suggests, Quaker pedagogy is neither teacher-centered nor student-centered, but subject-centered: teacher and students are jointly engaged in an inquiry into a third "great thing"—which "has a presence so real, so vivid, so vocal, that it can hold teacher and students alike accountable for what they say and do."[13] In the person of a sensitive and spiritually aware teacher, such an attitude is infectious and helps to set the tone in all but the most chaotic classrooms. Students themselves yearn for this deeper connection to a larger reality, and when they are assured of respectful and loving support, are more receptive to hearing its call—not only from the teacher, but also from others, and indeed, from their own hearts.

Thus Fox's probing query, "What canst thou say?" is not an invitation to shallow self-absorption, an indulgent shrinking of attention to the small span of one's momentary obsessions. Rather, it is an unsettling challenge to put ourselves on the line, to say what we know experientially of the larger world. Fox's question to his critics, and the pedagogical principle it inspires, call for humble opening to a reality to which we belong and to which we all must answer, whether we like it or not.

Although in most classrooms, teachers typically occupy center stage, the symbolism implied by this focus is both seductive and suspect. If teaching is the activity of helping people to learn, then the true focal points of an enlightened educational process are the learners themselves. Responsible teachers are attentive to their students, mindful of group dynamics, aware of subtle signals within the classroom, and ready to take into account the particular circumstances of their hearers that may affect the learning process. A concept that was originally developed for managerial and business ethics is useful here, that of "servant leadership." The author of this concept, Robert K. Greenleaf, was himself a Friend, and brought his Quaker beliefs to bear upon the analysis of effective leadership. A good leader takes care "to make sure that other people's highest priority needs are being served. The best test... is: Do those served grow as persons? Do they *while being served*, become healthier, wiser, freer, more autonomous, and more likely themselves to become servants? *And*, what is the effect on the least privileged in society: will they benefit, or, at least, not be further deprived?"[14]

Greenleaf summarizes a central feature of Quaker pedagogy: good teaching serves that of God in the learner, inviting and calling out the best, supporting the whole person. Good pedagogy does not pander to student self-indulgence, but rather invites students to serve others, in fuller engagement with their worlds. It does not preclude firmness, sternness, or even anger, if learners do not themselves recognize and honor their own sacredness. But a teacher's firmness should not arise from a bruised ego or fear of loss of control, but rather from dedication to the potential within the learner that is not being honored.

Nonviolence

Rather than seeing the classroom as battleground or boot camp, Quaker pedagogy accepts the invitation of William Penn, "Let us then try what love can do."[15] Coercion may secure grudging compliance with a teacher's demands; all too often, however, intimidation elevates fear to the primary pedagogical principle and drives learners away from their own Inward Teacher. Education becomes a dutiful command performance, backed by threat.

In contrast, Quaker pedagogy promotes respect for the unfolding consciousness within the learner. Although clear expectations for students are helpful (including an understanding of the consequences of failure), the primary pedagogical tone should be not intimidation but invitation and support, so that with appropriate help, students may quicken to the pure joy of seeing and knowing. Learning environments should be safe spaces in which all may drop defenses and open more fully to their shared endeavor.

But what of that ubiquitous, troubling feature of educational institutions, grades—and the coercion they imply? How can one reconcile the assignment of grades (with their power to punish or reward, arrogate or humiliate, certify or exclude) with Friends' testimonies of peace and love? Early Friends were not anarchists; their disavowal of the use of force was not absolute. While opposing war and preparation for war, they did not advocate the abolition of police, physical restraint, or legal punishment; rather, they assumed that to maintain public order required use of the sword to deter evildoers.[16] In our efforts to secure safety and good order, we should rely as much as possible upon gentler means and employ forcible restraint, confinement and other forms of punishment only when genuinely necessary. Even when force is used, every effort should be made to lovingly support the offender in walking a more orderly path.

In pedagogical matters, a similar understanding applies. Consistent truthfulness requires that we be prepared to speak not only truth that is pleasant to hear, but also (as the blunt, outspoken George Fox himself often displayed) to be truthful in ways that may be unwelcome and hard to hear, yet needed.

Grades may serve as honest assessments, providing feedback that is truthful if not always flattering. Brandishing the stick should never be the primary inducement to educational effort. But if all other attempts to reach a wayward student fail, it may be necessary to let the student experience the consequences of unacceptable behavior, whether through poor marks or other forms of discipline.

Actual practice at contemporary Quaker schools provides helpful perspective. A few dispense entirely with grades, relying upon oral and written comments. Most, however, employ grading systems similar to those used in non-Quaker institutions, not solely as judgments upon students' performance but also to communicate expectations and encourage better work; and all have some established means of disciplining students for their own good and for the good of the school. Unless we are drawn into abstract, polarized debate, there is no contradiction between avoiding coercion as much as possible, and employing tough love such as low grades or other disciplinary measures as needed.

Conclusion

Quaker pedagogy is a work in progress; it continues to evolve as Quaker educators realize the deeper implications of their faith and practice, while adapting to ongoing change and shifting circumstance. I have highlighted five strands of Quaker pedagogy:

- **The priority of experience:** Awaken fully to our encounters with the world.
- **Integrity:** Link education consistently with the whole of life.
- **The facts are friendly:** Trust that creation is welcoming and life-affirming.
- **Invite all voices:** Include all in the community of learning.

- **Nonviolence:** Respect the tender souls of teachers and learners alike.

These do not by any means exhaust the scope of pedagogical principles inspired by Friends' spiritual life. They do, however, provide a preliminary touchstone for self-examination, as educators seek to unite professional and personal lives within a larger, encompassing purpose: to support our students and ourselves as all grow stronger, more loving, and more knowing of that which deserves our ultimate attention and care.

Part III:

UNION

CHAPTER SEVEN

IN THE LOVE OF NATURE

Coming Home

Beneath my bare feet, the soft clods of Iowa loam sink beneath my weight, crumbling into a moist, living cushion. Each step is excruciatingly delicious, a pleasure almost too intense to bear. If I had reached into the chest of my mother and held her living, beating heart in the palm of my hand, my sensations could not have been more intimate or intense.

Recent rains have given way to an azure sky swept by plump cumulus clouds. The air is cool, fresh, expectant. I am eight years old. A few minutes ago, the bus from my rural elementary school deposited me at the foot of the driveway to our two-story white clapboard farmhouse. Stepping from the bus, I heard our International Harvester Farmall tractor, a quarter of a mile away. Running up the driveway to the house, I burst into the kitchen and asked my mother:

"Mama, what is Daddy doing?

"Oh, Irving is plowing. Thee can run down and see him, if thee wants."

133

Hurrying down the lane to one of our best fields—fifteen acres of flat ground, amply fertilized, with good drainage, the topsoil deep and fecund—I see my father in the distance, hunched over the steering wheel of the Farmall, his eyes fixed upon the unfolding furrow beneath him. The plowing is nearly complete. Before me lies a vast expanse of jumbled black velvet—gloriously rich soil, teeming with insects and worms that have been abruptly evicted from subterranean darkness and laid bare to the unforgiving glare of the sun. This rich harvest of tiny, delectable beings has seemingly attracted every bird within miles.

Pausing by fence-posts at the corner of the field, I kick off my shoes and socks and walk across the field toward my father—and as I do, I invade the ongoing avian orgy. Waves of flight rise up before me—meadowlarks, bobolinks, robins, sparrows, flickers, red-winged blackbirds—and grackles, black with iridescent green and blue highlights. Swirling away from my advancing figure, the birds promptly alight at a distance to resume their greedy feast. All is sensation: the shuddering thrill of my toes sinking into a black carpet, breeze caressing my skin, the visual wonder around me. No worries cloud my consciousness; I have "lost my mind and come to my senses."

So long as I exist, this memory will be a part of me. An old rural maxim says, "You can take the boy out of the farm—but you can't take the farm out of the boy." Yet as I reflect back upon this moment of ecstasy, my nostalgia is tinged with irony and sadness. Before it is plowed, the topsoil is interlaced with a network of tiny roots and particles that hold it in place, retarding erosion. The double-bottom plow pulled by the Farmall lifts a continuous slab of earth and dumps it upside down, exposing an underbelly of clods and the countless tiny lives that sought refuge in them. After plowing come disking and harrowing, further reducing large clods to an even crumble that is suitable for mechanical planting. Stored biotic energy is freed to fuel an explosion of crops that are chosen to satisfy human interests, while drawing down the soil's reserves. One hundred fifty years of continuous cultivation have depleted topsoil depth and fecundity that had accumulated over millennia. Describing our farm, Margaret Smith Lacey writes that "the spring reveals more and more black topsoil washing down into the slough, to tiny Coal Creek, to the Skunk River, to the Mississippi, to lie in the mouth of the Father of Waters where it opens into the Gulf of Mexico, at long last nothing but sludge."[1] Mindful of this depletion, my father was one of the first farmers in our county to plow and plant hilly land on the contour so that rows of corn and soybeans were at right angles to the downward slopes, thus reducing run-off. He also created terraces in some fields to further limit loss of topsoil. Still, these measures did not halt (much less reverse) the erosion, but merely slowed it. Sixty years after my walk across that fifteen acre field, many farmers now use minimum tillage, a practice that disturbs the topsoil only enough to permit planting. Minimum tillage sets no unlimited feasts for grackles.

I likened my sensation of walking across a plowed field to holding the beating heart of my mother in the palm of my hand. Although gruesome, this image is apt. The part of Mother Earth constituting our small family farm was the source of our sustenance and comfort. Much of the food that we ate was home-grown—and the farm's grain and alfalfa fed our livestock, whose sale in turn provided most of our meager income. The farm's topsoil was literally the ground of our lives. My father's plow gashed its skin, laying its unguarded bounty bare to the sky; in such intimacy is also great vulnerability. To preserve and protect the earth's treasures, we need at times to withdraw at a distance from them.

How difficult it is, to draw back from that which one loves! Yet when the loved one is ailing, perhaps a delicate invalid, we know that we must approach with mindfulness and care. Our profligate consumption of natural goods is, after all, the driving cause of our growing ecological crisis. Only when we approach the earth with humility and respect, may we find balance that leads to an earth restored.

The title of this chapter comes from the first line of a poem composed by the 19th-century American poet, William Cullen Bryant. The poem, "Thanatopsis," is a meditation upon nature and death. Its first eight lines are as follows:

> To him who in the love of nature holds
> Communion with her visible forms, she speaks
> A various language; for his gayer hours
> She has a voice of gladness, and a smile,
> And eloquence of beauty, and she glides
> Into his darker musings, with a mild
> And healing sympathy, that steals away
> Their sharpness, ere he is aware... .

Bryant was seventeen years of age when he completed the poem, prompting his first critics to doubt that he was the true author. At a similar age, I discovered the poem, fell in love with it, and memorized it for a high school English class. What I loved about the poem then were not Bryant's reflections upon death and dying, but rather his evocation of vast, uncharted wilderness. Frequently wounded by social interactions, I was (and still am) a lover of solitude; immersion in a peaceful pastoral scene is a balm for my broken spirit. Half a century later, I now appreciate Bryant's intertwining of death and natural beauty. "Thanatopsis" contains no hints of a growing ecological crisis; for him, nature remains vast and inexhaustible:

> ..."Take the wings
> Of morning, pierce the Barcan wilderness,
> Or lose thyself in the continuous woods

Where rolls the Oregon, and hears no song
Save his own dashings... .

Yet today one can hardly think of the natural world without simultaneously evoking images of depletion, death, and dying. Global warming, glacial melt and shrinking aquifers, destruction of vast swathes of tropical rain forest, poisoning of atmosphere, waterways and ocean, diminished fish stock, desertification, the extinction of countless species—these and other signs of natural morbidity press in upon awareness, darkening our joy in natural beauty with elegiac sadness. We are losing the very reality that sustains our spirit. In *Walden*, Henry David Thoreau declared "the tonic of wildness" to be a natural human need:

At the same time that we are earnest to explore and learn all things, we require that all things be mysterious and unexplorable, that land and sea be infinitely wild, unsurveyed and unfathomed by us because unfathomable. We can never have enough of nature. We must be refreshed by the sight of inexhaustible vigor, vast and titanic features, the sea-coast with its wrecks, the wilderness with its living and its decaying trees, the thundercloud, and the rain which lasts three weeks, and produces freshets. We need to witness our own limits transgressed, and some life pasturing freely where we never wander.[2]

Of all the many tragic consequences of the present and growing ecological crisis, one of the most troubling is that we have come to doubt the "inexhaustible vigor" of the natural world, to question the very existence of unexplorable, unfathomable wildness. Thirty years ago while on a backpacking trip into the High Sierras, after several days of hiking, I reached a spot seemingly so remote and untouched, so pristine and pure that I felt it had just come out of the hands of God. Then rounding a corner, I came upon a discarded beer can. What a falling off of wonder and joy! The human footprint is over all—a source of deep sorrow.[3]

What impels us as human beings to intrude and invade, to appropriate and dominate? And where do these compulsions lead us? For many years my thinking about the future of our small planet has been haunted by a simplistic yet terrifying image.

Making Hard Cider

In the mid-sixties, ten years before I give up the use of alcohol, I decide to try my hand at making hard cider. I buy a jug of apple juice, drop a handful of raisins into it, and then secure the top so that gases produced by fermentation can be released, while outside air does not penetrate into the brew. I place the jug on a warm windowsill and leave it there. The cider begins to bubble as bacteria introduced by the raisins reproduce exponentially, consuming natural sugars while releasing alcohol as a waste product. After several days the frenzied bubbling slows, then ceases. What has happened? The sugars have been largely exhausted—and the bacteria are dying off in their own waste. (The cider is, by the way, undrinkable. I taste it cautiously, then flush it down the toilet, disappointed.)

Like the jug of apple juice, Spaceship Earth (to use a phrase coined by Friend Kenneth Boulding) is a largely closed system in which a dominant species—ourselves—is rapidly multiplying, while consuming ever-greater quantities of non-renewable resources. The waste products produced by agriculture, industry, automobiles, and other human activities intrude upon the quality of life for the entire biosphere. Although non-human life and the poor of the earth suffer most from the poisoned ecosystem, even wealthy humans experience its effects. Behind the pattern of accelerating consumption and waste lies a compulsive pursuit of intoxication, an accelerating slide into system death.

As Mahlon Hoagland and Bert Dodson declare in *The Way Life Works*, "Humans exhibit addictive tendencies when trying to maximize such values as wealth, pleasure, security, and power.... Too much of a good thing is not a good thing."[4] Buddhist teacher Jack Kornfield articulates well the underlying malaise:

> In a society that almost demands life at double time, speed and addictions numb us to our own experience. In such a society, it is almost impossible to settle into our bodies or stay connected with our hearts, let alone connect with one another or the earth where we live. Instead, we feel ourselves increasingly isolated and lonely, cut off from one another and the natural web of life.... That is the most pervasive sorrow in our modern life.[5]

Many initiatives are essential in addressing the environmental crisis; none by itself is sufficient. There is no silver bullet that will restore the earth. Regarding the relative priorities of different factors, there is room for disagreement among informed and reasonable people: for example, some insist that our most critical step is to bring human population growth under control; others place top priority on the discovery and development of renewable sources of energy; yet others press for sustainable agriculture. Each of these initiatives is essential, along with many others. I am convinced, however, that we too quickly seek solutions outside of ourselves, overlooking the spiritual condition that lies at the root of it all: our acquisitive compulsion, driven by fear and greed. If we lived our lives in balance and peace, heedful of our inner guide—if, as John Woolman urged, we were "To turn all the treasures we possess into the channel of Universal Love"[6]—then our patterns of production, distribution, and consumption of material goods would harmonize with the life of the earth.

Many years ago I read that if one confines too many laboratory rats into too small a cage, they turn on one another—biting, scratching, and wounding, in spasms of desperation and fear. This image also has exercised a hold on my picture of human life upon earth. Spurred by gross inequality, perceived scarcity activates our lower natures, elevating suspicions and hatreds over tolerance, acceptance, and love. Nativistic fury in the United States regarding the influx of undocumented workers (so-called "illegal aliens") is one example of this atavistic response, as are countless conflicts arising from competition for scarce resources. The ecological crisis springs from a failure of faithfulness, compassion, and mutual trust. Scientific and technological developments may ease our dependence upon non-renewable resources and ameliorate the harm we do. Yet such developments will fail to achieve their ends if there is no change in the underlying dynamic of compulsive consumption and competitive self-gratification.

In Quaker perspective, the crisis of our earth has the same roots as conflict and war: unbridled pursuit of self-centered goals. When he affirmed what we now call the Quaker Peace Testimony, George Fox frequently cited a little book in the *New Testament,* "The Letter of James." In the language of the King James Version and of George Fox, James declares that the source of war is lust. Rendered in contemporary English, the key passage is as follows:

> Those conflicts and disputes among you, where do they come from? Do they not come from your cravings that are at war within you? You want something and do not have it; so you commit murder. And you covet something and cannot obtain it; so you engage in disputes and conflicts. You do not have, because you do not ask. You ask and do not receive, because you ask wrongly, in order to spend what you get on your pleasures. (4:1-3)

James affirms that the correction for this condition of conflicts and disputes is to open to "the wisdom that is from above is first pure, then peaceable, gentle, and willing to yield, full of mercy and good fruits, without a trace of partiality or hypocrisy." (3:17)

The Wisdom from Above

Reduced to its simplest terms, the ecological crisis is a vast pattern of insufficient love: love of humans, love of non-human life, love of the earth itself, love of God.

This assertion may seem facile. Is it really true (as the Beatles sang) that "love is all you need"? Does not the healing of the earth require immense resources—of political will, technological development, education, enlightened economic policy, and much, much more? Yes, indeed. Yet all such initiatives will be undermined if our underlying motivations remain small and self-serving: our political initiatives will falter, technological development will be co-opted to gratify consumer impulses, education will become subverted—and so on. Despite the many competing prognostications of futurists, we cannot confidently formulate a privileged ideology that must guide us into our future. As Paul Hawken, one of the world's leading environmental activists, declares, "You can try to determine the future, or you can try to create conditions for a healthy future. To do the former, you must presume to know what the future should be. To do the latter, you learn to have faith in social outcomes in which citizens feel secure, valued, and honored."[7]

Hearing the voice of love requires careful discernment. During the last quarter-century, the earliest and most prophetic Quaker voice on the environment has been that of Marshall Massey, whose address to Pacific Yearly Meeting in 1985 and subsequent speech at Friends General Conference in 1987 may be fairly said to have "energized the entire North American Quaker community."[8] Massey has in recent years been somewhat less in the Quaker public eye, in part because of the many other Friends who have followed his lead in speaking out on environmental issues. Yet he remains one of the wisest, most spiritually-grounded and best-informed environmental thinkers in all of Quakerism. In an entry on his blog, "The EarthWitness Journal," he reflects on the relative priorities of advocacy, environmental education, and spiritual discernment, observing that

A person might have all the environmental education in the world, and yet still be too unconcerned about the lives and sufferings of the creatures that her choices are affecting to make any major changes in her lifestyle or her business decisions. (I can personally name dozens of friends, who all know better intellectually, who nevertheless add far more than their share to the global greenhouse gas build-up, by taking long airplane flights on vacation and for avoidable business purposes.) Education, and even accountability, do not guarantee that a person will care enough about generations to come to choose to do things differently... .

Addressing such wickedness means doing our best, not just to educate others about environmental matters, but, far more basically, to infect them with the fundamental sensitivities of heart and conscience that will deter them from doing such wrong things. And we do that best, I think, by helping them fall in love with the Inward Guide.

There are many others besides... Friends, who are advocating... and engaging in environmental education. Our help is needed in all these areas, but it's not as if we are the only ones who can do it.

But who, other than Friends, is genuinely interested in helping people to fall in love with the Inward Guide? I don't know of anyone at all.

So although I hope with all my heart that every single one of us is doing something meaningful in the areas of advocacy and environmental education,... nevertheless, when I listen unflinchingly, I find my heart telling me that...

we as Friends need above all to be working on drawing
people into a love relationship with the Inward Guide, because that alone can make wrongs like over-fishing, and
like both coal and nuclear power, feel so profoundly wrong
that no temptation can possibly draw them into sin."[9]

Among progressives everywhere, views about the environment are often heavily tinged with pessimism. Those looking
for a contrary, hopeful tone may wish to read Paul Hawken's
*Blessed Unrest: How the Largest Movement in the World Came
into Being and Why No One Saw It Coming*.[10] Hawken is all too
familiar with the deluge of data on ecological decline; yet perhaps more than any other living human being, he is aware of a
rising tide of constructive initiatives, an unprecedented "global
humanitarian movement arising from the ground up": "coher-
ent, organic, self-organized congregations involving tens of mil-
lions of people dedicated to change."[11] The groups and movements that constitute this blessed unrest often do not know of
their allies around the globe. Like a pot of water that begins to
simmer, each bubble arises as a response to a specific hot spot,
apart from other bubbles—yet because the whole pot is heating
simultaneously, these individual eruptions are the early signs of
what will soon be a rolling boil. Likewise, as the systemic threats
to planet earth spread, intersect, and reinforce each other, the
global crisis increasingly gives rise to a globalized response.
This is Hawken's largest movement in the world—a cause for
hope, not despair.

The Peace Testimony
in Earthcare Witness

My analogy fails in one important respect: if left on the
heat, water eventually boils away entirely, leaving only a dry
pot and possibly an even greater conflagration. Yet the blessed
unrest to which Hawken points is not merely an evaporation

into nothingness, but many creative efforts to reverse the over-heating. It is here that Friends' testimonies have the greatest relevance. If individual earthcare initiatives around the globe follow only local priorities, if they seek to maximize the interests of one group against another and thus sacrifice larger global health, then the picture is indeed bleak: the peoples of the earth will resemble rats in a confined space who turn on each other. The ecological crisis multiplies and magnifies sources of armed conflict around the globe. To meld the many disparate initiatives that Hawken identifies into a genuinely global movement for earthcare, what is needed is the largest effort at peacemaking and collaboration that the world has ever seen. This collaboration cannot be imposed from above by well-meaning philanthropists and foundations; it must arise from the grassroots and be fed by listening across boundaries, so that we learn to cooperate with wider and wider circles of concerned persons. Friends' historic testimony regarding peace and conflict resolution, with its emphasis upon listening to and respect for the other, positions us well to facilitate this effort.

To serve this larger cause, Friends must reach out in unprecedented ways. The distinctive subculture of Quakerism can be isolating, creating an illusion that only Friends stand for peace, justice, and an earth renewed. In my own yearly meeting sessions, discussions on unity with nature are often infected with insularity and naïve parochialism that arise from ignorance of allies in the larger environmental movement. Through creative adaptation of our traditional testimonies, Friends have much to offer this movement.[12]

A paradigm of Quaker contributions to constructive engagement and collaboration was the life and career of Gilbert White, who died in 2006. An internationally recognized geographer, White was a high-profile advocate for social and environmental justice and a recipient of many awards for his distinguished service, including the national Medal of Science, presented to him by President Clinton in 2000. President of Haverford College from 1946 to 1955, and chair of the American Friends Service Committee from 1963 to 1969, he was one of the strongest early voices in Quakerism on behalf of environmental causes. In White's work with non-Quaker individuals and organizations, he sought to "model by example his conviction that at least two basic precepts of Quakerism warranted reinterpretation and expanded application to help society address the grave environmental problems facing our times: first, the tenet of nonviolence; second, the Religious Society's commitment to discernment of a 'sense of the meeting' in decision making."[13]

White's use of Quaker process among very diverse constituencies was the source of much of his effectiveness. One of his admirers from the National Research Council on Sustainable Water Supplies for the Middle East (which White chaired) declared that "possibly only a Quaker could have created the mutual trust needed for that group to collaborate under such trying circumstances."[14]

Friends' collaborative model of group decision-making, in which all voices are welcomed in a context of mutual respect, safeguards against two activist pathologies that frequently infect the environmental movement: grandiosity and legalism. Grandiosity arises when one begins to feel that the entire course of the world depends upon one's own personal choices, as if one were the ruler of the universe. It is humbling to recognize that if every one of the more than 300,000 Friends in the world reduced his or her carbon footprint to zero, the combined effect of that Quakerly carbon reduction upon the total global accumulation of greenhouse gases would be negligible. One must approach the project of saving the world with humility.

Grandiosity also lurks within the second pathology: the legalistic mindset of what might be called eco-pharisees, who reduce earthcare to a set of rigid rules covering every aspect of life, with attendant guilt for the slightest infraction of those rules. A doctrinaire approach to eco-correctness alienates others, creating pushback that undermines effectiveness. The healing of the world will not come from self-righteous assumptions of eco-purity and denunciations of the failings of others, but from reaching out in love to discern a larger, all-encompassing unity.

Friends are fond of saying of Meeting for Worship for the Conduct of Business that the longer and more difficult the agenda, the more time should be allotted to worship. A similar contemplative logic applies to effective Quaker activism: the more urgent the issue, the greater the danger of inadequate discernment and a rushed response, hence the greater the need for settled wisdom arising from quiet reflection. Demonstrations on the streets and lobbying in the corridors of power are essential efforts—yet these are often inspired by work that is done in quieter settings. Henry David Thoreau, John Muir, Aldo Leopold, and Rachel Carson must surely be on any list of the most influential figures of the environmental movement of the past two centuries. Each was politically engaged, an activist for change; yet each gained access to public platforms of influence and power through the relatively private labor of writing and publishing that subsequently drew the attention of others. The greatest, most lasting contributions of these influential thinkers have come through the written word. What transforms the world is not simply feet on the street—but moral vision.

When environmental concerns become wholly politicized, an anxious tussle with the forces of depredation, then we surrender to the very conditions we abhor. What can save us from this self-induced defeat? Two things are necessary: first a humble recognition of our own complicity in the destruction of the earth: we are *all* ecological sinners who contribute to environmental decline. Measuring our own carbon footprint is a step toward shrinking it. And secondly, as Marshall Massey observes, we must reawaken to the Source of light, love, and beauty that alone can restore us to a right relationship with Creation, out of which true healing of the earth may come. These are key moments in the ancient mystical path: *purgation* (seeing plainly the truth of our lives, and emptying ourselves of self-centered attachment), and *illumination* (opening to the Light and allowing ourselves to be guided by it)—leading at last to the heart's true desire: *union*.

Quakerism is well positioned to assume a central role in this process of ecological redemption. Contemporary Friends often do not appreciate the distinctive theological gifts bequeathed to us by our Quaker foremothers and forefathers. For the Puritan Calvinists (among whom Quakerism came into being), the created world was fraught with evil and corruption; only a spiritualized transcendence of that world by the grace of God could yield redemption. Against those Puritan "professors" who insisted that "all was sin," George Fox stoutly declared the possibility of redemption and perfection in *this* life—and in *this* world. In his great religious opening of 1648, Fox awakened to a state of "pureness, and innocency, and righteousness" and then "into a state in Christ Jesus, that should never fall"—and also simultaneously into an entrancing reconnection with the created world, which "gave another smell unto me than before, beyond what words can utter... the creation was opened to me."[15] These two dimensions of Fox's awakening are inseparable: intimacy with God—and intimacy with Creation. Genuine faithfulness to one is essentially linked to faithfulness to the other. Among the many diverse versions of Christian theology, Quaker religious thought is among the most earth-friendly and adaptable to an ecological age.

Awakening to Natural Presence

Few of us read theology for edification and enjoyment, however. What does the earth-friendly tenor of early Quaker thought mean for our daily spiritual practice? It means, first of all, that we should not draw a sharp line between the practice of waiting upon the Spirit, and that of opening to Presence in Nature. It means that even as we make the pragmatic choices to bring our patterns of consumption into harmony with a sustainable future and advocate for earth-sensitive legislation and policy, we also need to support these practical efforts by a spiritual discipline that returns us to intimacy with the natural world. By what perverse logic do we imagine that we can restore the earth while we ourselves remain alienated from her? As Gerald G. May writes, "We can never begin to heal the damage we have done to the earth until our own souls find a way back to being who they are as part of the Nature we so care for... (I)t is Nature Herself who must heal our wound and turn us toward wholeness."[16] In a series of contemplative meditations upon a massive "matriarch tree," May evokes this experience of intimacy with extraordinary clarity and power:

When my comments cease and my symbols evaporate and my feelings dissolve into pure Presence, I join the tree in its real, immediate being. What I feel is not emotion but sheer perception: the touch of breeze on my skin, the pressure of ground on my feet, my heart's pulse... . I am, for the moment at least, in the fullness of life.

This is the wilderness of being. It is what Wisdom showed me, where Nature has always taken me. It is Her home, Her dwelling, the place of Her abiding, the sacred household of being-as-it-is where all creation is at home in its wildness... and nothing is domesticated.[17]

The healing of self is also the healing of the world:

Wisdom calls and leads me into my own nature, wordlessly encouraging me to be natural... . It is home, my true home, the hearth of my spirit.

It is when I am in this abiding-place that everything comes together: experience and concept, beauty and truth, senses and thoughts, responses and comments, primal being and scientific knowledge. They all become one being, one experience, one appreciation, one sparkle in the radiance of being alive.[18]

Contemplative immersion in the natural world—sensing the wonder of life—dispels the noxious fumes of self-centered thought and awakens us to our true nature. In a thoughtful essay, Friend Ellen Ross echoes these themes:

> Living in the presence of our Earth-connections provides people with personal sustenance and meaning, and, even more, it often empowers people to advocate for environmental well-being as well.

> I believe that one of the important ways to slow the relentless destruction of the natural world is for us to live in compassionate mindfulness of the places we love. We must remember the spaces we care about: what they look like, smell like, sound like, what colors we see, and how we feel when we are there. We must feel deeply the specialness of these places. For many of us, it is only when we feel again the comfort, the oneness, the beauty, the joy, the calm, the delight, and even at times the grief of the loss of these spaces, that energy will well up within us to protect these lands and these experiences for generations to come.[19]

Awareness of natural presence dispels another temptation of environmental activism: anthropocentrism, the disposition to see all environmental issues in terms of exclusively human self-interest. The debate about global warming, for example, is often framed merely in terms of threats to human beings—inundation of coastal cities, the destruction of agriculture, and loss of tourist destinations. When all of non-human nature is viewed only as a resource and means to human ends, we revert to the very mind-set that has brought us and the earth into crisis. Aldo Leopold observed that we need a land ethic that "changes the role of *Homo Sapiens* from conqueror of the land community to plain member and citizen of it. It implies respect for his fellow-members, and also respect for the community as such."[20]

A Hidden Blessing

There is no place that does not see you. You must change your life.

—Rilke

Humans have a capacity that is not shared by bacteria in a jug, or rats in a cage: the capacity for gratitude. What is gratitude? It is the recognition that one has received a gift, and the loving acknowledgment of that gift. Gratitude is fostered by generosity—the generosity of loved ones, the generosity of strangers, the generosity of the earth, the generosity of God. Generosity invites gratitude; and gratitude in turn fosters greater generosity. As we enlarge the scope of our concern beyond our small selves, we grow into a larger, loving communion. We need a post-partisan politics and a post-partisan spirituality that are large and generous in Spirit, reaching out to more of those in need—not only to ourselves and other humans, but to all of life on earth, and indeed, to the earth itself. Concerns regarding the environment are inseparable from concerns regarding justice— and justice must encompass *all* of life.

Are we ready for such transformation of the mind and spirit? Are we willing to take the risk of opening to greater clarity and insight? Traditional Christian language calls such transformation metanoia and sees it as essential to salvation. Efforts to care for the earth will find their true power when we know—not as a matter of intellect, or even of emotion, but in our bones—how we must live. As George Fox never tired of declaiming, the Light is within us now, always available if we but awaken to it.

David Korten declares,

Everything is going to change. The question is whether

we let the changes play out in increasingly destructive ways or embrace the deepening crisis as our time of opportunity. Now as never before we must unleash the creative potential of the species and direct it to democratizing our cultures and institutions and bringing ourselves into balance with one another and Earth. It is the greatest creative challenge the species has ever faced. Success would seem a futile dream, except that all around the planet momentum is already building.[21]

Global trends are terrifying, yet there is a hidden blessing in these trends as well: they will require us to look deeply into ourselves, perhaps more deeply than ever before: they will require us to seek God. It is helpful to remember that Quakerism did not arise in a time of relative peace and domestic tranquility, but in a 17th-Century England that was riven by turmoil, unrest, civil war, and political conflict, a world "turned upside down."[22] Would as vigorous a religious movement have arisen in more peaceful times? Or was that 17th-Century cauldron of chaos a stimulus for the passion and inner fire of early Friends? Spirituality often burns most brightly under conditions of chaos, dislocation, and injustice. In Nazi prisons and death camps, in the squalor of barrios in Latin America, in the "City of Joy"[23] in Calcutta, spiritual faith may shine with a more vital, illuminating flame than it does within the comfortably complacent communities of the first world.

Even for those of us who live in such first-world communities, it becomes more difficult to shut ourselves off from larger global realities. This is surely one of the benefits of that very mixed bag called "globalization": we see more clearly the actual conditions of life around the globe, human and non-human. As the world becomes smaller and more transparent, more effort is required to remain blind to suffering and injustice; in the end, such constricted blindness must fail. And in that failure, lies hope for us all. As Friends, we are called to take the greatest risk possible: to stand in the Light and recognize that we are known through and through—and to act out of that apocalypse of Truth. As we become faithful to the wisdom within us, we find that our lives increasingly settle into joyful harmony with Nature and God.

My own life has shown me that I must face the darkness if I am to open to the Light. My struggles with addiction, depression, divorce, and despair have given me the greatest gifts that I enjoy. In a life that is filled with blessings, all that I now treasure would have been impossible if I had not looked into the abyss and seen what I had become. Only then did my life change for the better.

A similar dynamic governs our ecological future. The choice that we face is stark: continuing down a path of blindness, destruction, and death—or opening to Truth, and acting accordingly. It is a choice that we face in each moment of each day, in countless small acts that either darken the future for ourselves, for our children, and for our children's children—or offer light and hope.

The God-drenched earth that humans are crucifying continues to offer itself to all of life—and within that sacrificial offering, lies the promise of redemption. We can find the courage to transform our habits of consumption, to advocate for progressive policies and legislation, and to work constructively with our progressive global allies when we take the risk to awaken to the Christ-Spirit that is within all things, awaiting our loving acceptance. Hearing that voice, our hearts, like that of George Fox, indeed do leap for joy.[24] Though a future of daunting challenges lies before us, all is not lost. As we learn to live in the love of nature, we may find comfort in the closing lines of Bryant's "Thanatopsis":

> ...Sustained and soothed
> By an unfaltering trust, approach thy grave
> Like one who wraps the drapery of his couch
> About him, and lies down to pleasant dreams.

CHAPTER EIGHT

JOYFUL WITNESS

The place God calls you to is the place where your deep gladness and the world's deep hunger meet.

—Fredrick Buechner[1]

If you want others to be happy, practice compassion. If you want to be happy, practice compassion.

—The Dalai Lama[2]

The Valley of Love and Delight

As I settle into a quiet morning of reflection and writing, the doorbell rings. A friend needs a ride, then a pick-up later in the day—can I possibly help? My mind races through a gamut of concealed emotions— disappointment at the interruption; sympathy for my friend's plight and gratitude for how politely he asks; then an immediate decision: "Yes, of course!"

Was my "Yes" wholehearted? What began as feigned enthusiasm quickly becomes the real thing. Having responded to my friend's need, I immediately

*sense his relief and gratitude. I taste the pleasure of
our mutual affection. As my ambivalence fades, I realize that the choice to help my friend is best not only
for him—but also for me. I enjoy our time together, and
when I return to writing, I discover an unanticipated
bonus. Before the doorbell rang, I had been staring at
a blank sheet of paper, puzzling over how to begin this
chapter. The doorbell derailed that puzzlement. Now
I see my way forward: responding to my friend's request has brought an unexpected gift in the form of a
simple parable that provides my opening here.*

Dorothy Day, American social activist and co-founder of
the Catholic Worker movement, called such moments "the
duty of delight."[3] Day invoked this phrase as a reminder to
respond gladly to the pressing needs of the poor, the hungry
and homeless, and the addicted and mentally ill who sought her
help. Day set what seems an impossibly high standard, but must
we respond with delight to every claim that others make upon
us? Is not the very phrase "the duty of delight" an oxymoron?
"Duty" feels burdensome and constraining, while "delight"
suggests weightless freedom. Is not duty the enemy of joy?

There is, of course, a vast gulf between my single modest
decision to help my friend, and Day's lifetime of heroic service.
Yet the cases illustrate a common theme, the systematic
delusion of self-centered thinking: pursuit of my apparent self-interest often isolates me from others; when habitually pursued, it
leads to an empty, disappointing life. In contrast, when I enlarge
the scope of my concern to include others' well-being and act accordingly, I find that my own life is enriched in unexpected ways.

How can we explain this apparent paradox? When I am
obsessed with my private desires, my vision narrows and my dis-
satisfaction is magnified, causing me to ignore others—whereas
when I see myself as one among many, I regain a balanced
and healthier view. As the Buddhist teacher Bodhipaksa notes,

learning of the pain of others puts my own concerns in perspective, undercutting inflated self-expectations and promoting contentment with my condition. (This truth is enshrined in the familiar proverb, "I complained because I had no shoes, until I met a man who had no feet.") Furthermore, focusing only upon myself obscures the degree to which I am a social being, whereas compassionate giving reawakens me to my intrinsic bonds with others. Bodhipaksa continues, "Compassion and love give our lives a sense of meaning and fulfillment, and compassion is inherently pleasurable and rewarding. When we are caught up in our own anxieties and longings we are not fully able to connect with others and so our experience is impoverished. Compassion is therefore enriching."[4]

The counsel to shift from narrow self-interest to concern for others is easily distorted into unhealthy self-denial, however. Historically, such self-denial has often been rationalized by an otherworldly theology that calls for repudiation of the body. In Christian and Hindu traditions, asceticism has sometimes taken the form of deliberate mortification of the body as a sign of spiritual devotion.

A more pervasive pattern of unhealthy self-denial arises from the oppression of women. The expectation that women should subordinate their interests to men is a defining principle of patriarchy, rationalizing exploitation in the name of noble self-sacrifice. Because women in nearly all cultures bear disproportionate responsibility for childcare, and because parenting brings an endless procession of scenarios in which one must decide between satisfying one's personal wishes or responding to a child's demands, the pressure to set aside self-care can feel like a trap from which there is no escape. Attending to one's personal needs is experienced as a moral failure. Those who aspire to be "good mothers" may forget themselves entirely and live solely through their families. In the face of these pressures, it is not surprising if meeting one's needs comes to be expressed in unhealthy and manipulative ways.

While the assertion that "You must love yourself before you can love others" (and its variant, "You have to be at peace with yourself before you can make peace in the world") is often used to justify insular complacency that ignores the suffering of others, it nevertheless encapsulates an essential truth.

Like virtually all traditional cultures, Buddhism has been patriarchal in practice and has not been free of unhealthy self-abnegation. Yet in Buddhism's founding myth, Siddhartha Gautama claimed to have discovered a "Middle Way" between self-denial and self-indulgence, affirming healthy self-care. The founding teachings of Buddhism lend themselves naturally to gender equality. Bodhipaksa explains that while compassion for others tends toward our own happiness,

> This doesn't mean that we should neglect ourselves and be concerned only with others. Compassion for others is ideally an extension of a healthy self-cherishing attitude in which we take our own needs seriously. In Buddhist practice compassion is developed for all beings, including ourselves, and in fact meditations such as the *metta bhavana* (development of loving-kindness) and *karuna bhavana* (development of compassion) we begin by cultivating love towards ourselves.[5]

Christianity has a decidedly checkered history regarding the balance of self-care and care for others. I content myself here with the simple reminder that Jesus commands us "to love your neighbor as yourself," not "love your neighbor *instead of* yourself." (Mark 12:31—emphasis added)

Finding meaning and satisfaction through uniting wholeheartedly with a higher purpose is not confined to any religious or cultural heritage; the insight that human well-being depends upon devotion to a larger cause appears in many settings. Mihaly Csikszentmihalyi, a secular scientist and an internationally recognized pioneer in the new field of "positive psychology," declares,

"One cannot lead a life that is truly excellent without feeling that one belongs to something greater and more permanent than oneself... . Active responsibility for the rest of humankind, and for the world of which we are a part, is a necessary ingredient of a good life."[6] A similar sentiment was voiced by George Bernard Shaw:

> This is the true joy in life, the being used for a purpose recognized by yourself as a mighty one; the being thoroughly worn out before you are thrown on the scrap heap; the being a force of Nature instead of a feverish selfish little clod of ailments and grievances complaining that the world will not devote itself to making you happy.[7]

The link between one's own well-being and concern for others is explored in Stephen Post and Jill Neimark's *Why Good Things Happen to Good People: The Exciting New Research that Proves the Link Between Doing Good and Living a Longer, Healthier, Happier Life*. Their opening chapter begins: "If I could take one word with me into eternity, it would be 'give'... . (G)iving is the most potent force on the planet."[8] They continue:

> You wish to be happy? Loved? Safe? Secure? You want to turn to others in tough times and count on them? You want the warmth of true connection? You'd like to walk into the world each day knowing that this is a place of benevolence and hope? Then I have one answer: give. Give daily, in small ways, and you will be happier. Give and you will be healthier. Give, and you will even live longer.[9]

In the Abrahamic traditions, the joy of living as we should is expressed in theistic language. Affirming the delight of doing God's will, the Psalmist proclaims that "the ordinances of the Lord are true and righteous altogether. More to be desired are they than gold, even much fine gold; sweeter also than honey and drippings of honeycomb." (Psalm 19:9-10) This sentiment is echoed in the familiar lines of the beloved Shaker song, "Simple

Gifts." Whether caring for others or for ourselves, whether acting from simple kindness or out of passion for justice, we must first:

> ...Come down where we ought to be
> And when we find ourselves in the place just right,
> T'will be in the valley of love and delight.

Fighting for Peace and Justice

In the Judeo-Christian tradition, however, we are called not only to "love kindness," but also to "do justice" (Micah 6:8), and the work of justice seems to call for a sterner voice than does the simple commandment to love one another. When practiced within unjust political and social structures, compassion seemingly does not go to the root of the problem and may even serve to perpetuate injustice by softening its superficial features. In the West, the call for justice has traditionally been rooted in the prophetic books of the Hebrew scriptures, which are full of condemnation of the moral and spiritual failings of Israel. Yet here as well, doing what is right is typically depicted as not burdensome but joyful, holding out a promise of healing and redemption.

That witnessing for peace and justice need not be burdensome or self-righteous became clear to me in the summer of 1970, when I visited my parents in Honolulu. On the occasion of the 25th anniversary of the bombing of Hiroshima and Nagasaki, local Quakers had planned a peace march to a nearby U.S. military command center to protest the installation of nuclear weapons in the Pacific theater. We were pleased to find that we would be joined by Japanese Buddhist monks who were traveling the globe for peace in remembrance of the devastation of their homeland in 1945.

On the morning of the march the monks showed up in brightly-colored robes, bearing bold banners and large drums. Next to this festive display, we sober Friends were distinctly drab.

A few minutes into our march, a warm tropical rain began to fall. Soon we were all drenched. Quakers and Buddhists responded in strikingly differing ways. The Friends slogged through the downpour with a grave air of diffident self-importance, maintaining our pose as thoughtful citizens who were determined to make a weighty public statement. In contrast, the monks saw how ridiculous we were, laughing even as they celebrated peace and harmony. Which of us—the solemn, self-important Quakers or the laughing Buddhists—better served world peace?

Did the monks' laughter betray a superficial attitude toward their cause? Did it suggest that they had undertaken their pilgrimage "just for fun"? Searing images of Hiroshima and Nagasaki had been lodged deeply within Japanese cultural memory for a quarter of a century; that collective memory was, after all, the reason for the monks' journey. They had invested more of themselves—their material, psychological, and spiritual resources—than had we Quakers. Yet there was a disarming quality in the monks' manner that was absent from the Friends' solemn self-display. As I noted this contrast, my mind went back to a children's game of my youth, with its defining jingle: "Quaker Meeting has begun/No more laughing, no more fun." To play the game, we sat silently in a circle and put on solemn faces. To giggle or smile was to lose; anyone showing the slightest merriment must drop out. The "best Quaker" was the most sober, impassive child.

Prior to the march, Friends had held a weekly one-hour silent vigil on the campus of the University of Hawaii in Manoa to protest the Vietnam War. Participating in one of those vigils, I saw a variety of responses from those who passed by. Some applauded or gave "thumbs-up"; a few actually joined our ranks. Most ignored us; a few were visibly hostile. But our subdued public witness apparently did not impinge deeply upon the consciousness of most observers. We were too easy to dismiss. In contrast the monks on our peace march could not be ignored.

Their color and self-deprecating laughter invited curiosity, sympathy, and genuine engagement.

I do not suggest that levity must infuse all work for peace and justice. Effective witness takes countless forms; what is appropriate depends upon the circumstances. Experienced change agents cultivate sensitivity to the moment—including awareness of prevailing cultural norms, the particular gifts of those who act, and much more. Attentiveness to the unique situation is the cornerstone of *upaya*, the Buddhist concept of "skillful means." In their light-hearted and unpretentious adaptability, the monks displayed this virtue.

The monks reminded me once again that the effort to promote real change can be infused with joy, a "deep gladness" in doing what I am called to do. This gladness does not mean that such work is easy; on the contrary, it may be challenging, even painful. Often I must be ready to step outside of my comfort zone. Yet when I do work that is both appropriate to the moment and calls forth my best efforts (including strengths of which I was unaware), then I am blessed by a melding of my will with a larger positive purpose.

From Outrage to Gladness

In this world hatred is not dispelled by hatred; by love alone is hatred dispelled. This is an eternal law.

—*Dhammapada*[10]

In the heat of a painfully partisan political season, I hear a speech that affirms all of my own biases, and more. The speaker summarizes economic data with rapid-fire mastery and offers tidbits of political intrigue that confirm my darker suspicions. His conclusions flesh out my own prejudices in satisfying fullness. While he acknowledges the errors of our shared political heroes, these candid admissions are swamped

*by his damning indictment of our common enemies.
Soaking up his rhetoric, I swell with righteous indignation; surely I and my political compatriots are on the
side of justice, mercy, and sweet reason. Those who
oppose us are rigid, selfish ideologues.*

*Yet with this gratifying reassurance comes disqui-
et—a hint of caution and self-doubt. I notice that my
heart has hardened. My self-righteousness is shad-
owed by fear of those who oppose me. I am eager to
prevail over the enemies of mercy and justice.*

*This experience reminds me of another that oc-
curred years before: on a street corner in Santa Moni-
ca, California during the first Iraq War, I am part of an
anti-war demonstration. The longer I demonstrate, the
more my outrage escalates. Despite our outward civil-
ity, I am left with a disturbing aftertaste. My sleep that
night is troubled by dreams of violence against the op-
pressors—acts that in the light of day I would not seri-
ously consider. Taking part in an orderly public display for peace has paradoxically aroused me to hatred.
The only satisfactory antidote I can find for my toxic
reaction is to become quiet, to return to a still center
where I am able to sense my shared humanity with
those whose views differ from my own.*

No one with a tender and open heart can fail to be dis-
turbed by economic injustice, racism, sexism, human traffick-
ing, torture, exploitation, and the unfolding environmental holo-
caust—to say nothing of everyday suffering and untimely death.
Upon opening the newspaper or hearing network news, or merely
peeking beneath the deceptive calm and normality of our own
communities, anyone with a minimal concern for others must
taste despair. At such moments, we understand why humans
resort to violence; if we are honest with ourselves, we feel the
heat of outrage. Such emotional reactions are entirely human;

to be immune to them is to be either psychopathic or blind. Sensitivity to suffering and injustice is found in every awakened human heart.

Yet outrage is not a reliable mark of one's prophetic calling. We *should* be troubled by injustice, but when outrage prompts us to act impulsively, we deepen conflict rather than ease it. Claiming exclusive ownership of the "high ground," we demonize our opponents, hardening their resolve. Indulging in self-righteousness, we generate "push-back" from those we attack. In war propaganda and polarized political rhetoric, emotional reactivity blossoms full-blown, infiltrating everyday discourse, inspiring spiteful gossip and demeaning judgments. Claiming the moral high ground, we reject "the other." Paul Knitter, Professor of Theology, World Religions and Culture at Union Theological Seminary and author of the provocatively-titled *Without Buddha I Could Not Be a Christian*, writes,

> Actions that impose or force change upon that which is denounced as unjust and evil are, in a limited but real sense, violent. And according to the laws of physics and the psyche, a violent force will bring forth a counter-violent force. For the human psyche, this is so because violence communicates hatred. If the oppressors feel that they are being hated, if they feel that they are not being listened to or respected, they will respond with the all-too-human reaction of self-protection or violent hatred in return. Even if those who are demanding justice and denouncing oppression do not harbor hatred in their hearts (that is indeed a big "if"!) that will not be the message the denounced oppressors receive. Violence, willy-nilly, communicates hatred. And being hated reacts with violence.[11]

Knitter summarizes the point: "Just social structures require reconciled human hearts."[12]

A Deeper Unity

An enemy is one whose story we have not heard.

—Gene Knudsen Hoffman
Quaker mystic and activist[13]

Yet how can our hearts be reconciled with our awareness of the overwhelming brokenness and suffering of the world? How can we feed the hungry, heal the wounded, restore justice, and dry the ocean of tears without ourselves descending into anguish? How can such service possibly be "sweeter than honey and drippings of honeycomb"?

My engagement with Zen has helped me to see resources within my own Quaker tradition to meet this challenge. Friends are fond of quoting a phrase from George Fox, affirming "that of God in every one": a spring of spiritual insight exists in all persons, no matter how obscured. All effective social change begins with an appeal to that inner wisdom, which Buddhist writers call "Buddha-nature." Pema Chodron calls such an appeal "communication from the heart." It is grounded in humility and loving kindness toward oneself and others:

> To the degree that we trust ourselves, we have no need to close down on others. They can evoke strong emotions in us but still we don't withdraw. Based on this ability to stay open, we arrive at... the difficult-to-come-by fruition: the ability to put others before ourselves and help them without expecting anything in return.[14]

If these Buddhist sentiments sound familiar to Christians, it is because similar counsel is found in Christian scripture, notably in Jesus' admonition to "Love your enemies."

Beneath our differences, deeper than the conflicts that divide us, lies a common humanity. What does this familiar phrase mean? It means that we share with one another more than our common classification as members of the species, *homo sapiens*, and that we are all embraced in a larger whole, belonging to what George Fox called "the hidden unity in the Eternal Being."[15] How can we discern that hidden unity and replace mistrust with sincere acceptance and loving connection? Reconciliation across conflict begins with an act of faith, a willingness to trust that each human being carries within himself or herself the possibility of goodness. As we hear one another's stories, suspending our judgment and listening with an open heart, we discover what we share, and fear gradually yields to trust.

My favorite example of this wisdom comes from the writings of Margaret Fell, the founding mother of Quakerism. In 1654, during a time of domestic chaos and civil war in England, the fledgling Quaker movement was gathering momentum and facing harsh persecution from civil authorities, including beatings, imprisonment, and impounding of property. In response, Margaret Fell (later to marry George Fox) appealed "To Friends in the North" to provide material aid for needy Friends.[16] As far as I have been able to determine, Fell's appeal was historically the first corporate Quaker relief initiative, thus becoming an implicit model for future generations of relief work.

In her appeal, Margaret Fell might have emphasized the grievous sufferings of Quaker missionaries, stirring up indignation and outrage. She did not do this. Instead, she reminded Friends of a higher, more sustainable ground of action: their unity in the body of Christ. Lifting up the image of "the whole Body full of Light," Fell urged Friends to:

> Be subject, and obedient, to give freely up to the service of the body which is one... . And now, that nothing may be kept back, but as you have received freely, so freely... suffer for the body's sake... . (W)here one member suffers, all the members may suffer with it... . (R)emember those that are in bonds, (that you are) bound with them... . (B)ear one another's burdens and be equally yoked in the sufferings... . So my dear brethren and sisters, let brotherly

love continue, that every one, as the Lord moves you
and opens your heart... may come into the oneness in all
things, and in that abide which dwells in love and unity.[17]

In keeping with the volatile temper of the times, Margaret Fell
could be vituperative in her condemnation of injustice; yet when
she seeks the support of Friends on behalf of a mission of com
passion, she does not evoke fear and hatred. Rather, she calls
Friends to heed their better part, the voice of the Inward Teacher
that draws all into sacred unity in "the Body of Christ." She seeks
to include rather than exclude, to reach out rather than repudi-
ate, and to suffer for love's sake in a spirit of forgiveness and
compassion.[18]

John Woolman, the saintly eighteenth-century Quaker abolitionist, manifested this spirit to an extraordinary degree. As a
child he displayed an uncommonly tender, solicitous heart. As
he grew into a young man, Woolman's conscience was increasingly troubled by slavery. In 1758 he warned his fellow Quakers,

> My mind is often led to consider the purity of the Divine
> Being and the justice of his judgments, and herein my soul
> is covered with awfulness... . Many slaves on this continent
> are oppressed, and their cries have reached the ears of
> the Most High! Such is the purity and certainty of his judg-
> ments that he cannot be partial in our favour. In infinite
> love and goodness he hath opened our understandings
> from one time to another concerning our duty toward this
> people, and it is not a time for delay.[19]

Reading this prophetic opening, one might expect Woolman
to denounce slave-holding Friends. He was indeed persistent in
speaking out publicly against slavery, testifying that the cause
of righteousness is not advanced by remaining silent out of a
misplaced fear of offending. Justice requires that we bring our
witness to those who need to hear it. For example, when visiting
the homes of Quaker slaveholders to labor with them regarding the evils of slavery, Woolman's scruples would not allow him

to accept the service provided by slaves within that household without giving them coins in payment, a practice that discomfited the slaveholder.

Yet his witness was expressed in a remarkably gentle and loving manner. Both Woolman's determination to speak out and his kindness in doing so are reflected in the following passages from the *Journal*, in which he first affirms a duty to witness to the evils of slavery—and then immediately counsels loving kindness toward the slave-holders:

> To see the failings of our friends and to think hard of them, without opening that which we ought to open, and still carry a face of friendship—this tends to undermine the foundation of true unity... .

> To trade freely with oppressors and, without labouring to dissuade from such unkind treatment, seek for gain by such traffic tends, I believe, to make them more easy respecting their conduct than they would be if the cause of universal righteousness was humbly and firmly attended to... . I do not censure my brethren in these things, but believe the Father of Mercies, to whom all mankind by creation are equally related, hath heard the groans of these oppressed people and is preparing some to have a tender feeling of their condition.[20]

The gift of speaking clearly and honestly on behalf of justice without demonizing those who behave unjustly is also found in the remarkable public ministry of the 19th-century Quaker reformer, Lucretia Mott. An abolitionist and a feminist, Mott was courageous and unwilling to back down. She could be tart and direct, yet she did not indulge in scathing condemnation. Her husband, James, quieter and less public than his wife, supported her public witness. A fearless advocate for the rights of women, Mott nevertheless refrained from reverse gender prejudice, arguing that "We ought... to claim no more for woman than for man, we ought to put woman on a par with man, not invest her with power, or claim her superiority over her brother. If we do she is just as likely to become a tyrant as man is; as with Catherine the Second."[21]

In the 20th-century, the most dramatic example of urgent Quaker humanitarian outreach—dramatic because of the magnitude of the evil, the moral depravity of its perpetrators, and the audacity of the outreach itself—was a journey into Nazi Germany by three American Friends. In December 1938, just a month after the portentous events of *Kristallmacht*, three weighty Quakers, Rufus Jones, Robert Yarnall, and George Walton, crossed the Atlantic on a mission of mercy, hoping to gain some relief for German Jews. Jones, co-founder of the American Friends Service Committee and now almost 76 years old, had been one of the organizers of a massive effort to care for the survivors of World War I—first in France, then in Germany and Russia.[22] Prior to the trip, Jones had few illusions about their chances for success. He stated to Yarnall and Walton that "Nothing in the universe is so utterly unconquerable as a mind possessed by a set of ideas that have become entrenched and sacred."[23]

"The three wise men" (as the Quakers were sarcastically named by Goebbels before their arrival) had prepared a carefully worded written statement, making clear that their mission was wholly humanitarian and nonpartisan:

> We have come to Germany at this present time to see whether there might be any service which American Quakers could render, and to use every opportunity open to us to understand the present situation. ... (W)e have had close and friendly relations with the German people throughout the entire post-war period. ... We came to Germany in the time of the blockade; organized and directed the feeding of German children, reaching at the peak no less than a million two hundred thousand children per day... . In all this work we have kept entirely free of party lines or party

spirit. We have not used any propaganda or aimed to make converts to our own views. We have simply, quietly, and in a friendly spirit endeavored to make life possible for those who were suffering. We do not ask who is to blame for the trouble which may exist or what has produced the sad situation. Our task is to support and save life and to suffer with those who are suffering.[24]

The three Friends sought "speedy emigration on a large scale" for Jews—and in this regard they were in at least partial agreement with their German hosts, who had made an "implacable decision" that "the Jews must go." The initial response of the Gestapo to the Quakers' requests was seemingly favorable. Following a tension-filled discussion and (as the Gestapo hosts conferred outside the room) an impromptu Meeting for Worship ("the only Quaker Meeting ever held in the Gestapo!") the Nazi officers returned to announce, "Everything you have asked for is granted... . I shall telegraph tonight every police station in Germany that the Quakers are given full permission to investigate the sufferings of Jews and to bring such relief as they see necessary."[25] Yarnall recorded that this order included authorization to assist in Jewish emigration from Germany.

We now know that this seemingly far-reaching accord yielded only minimal humanitarian benefits. Clarence Pickett (who in 1929 became executive secretary of the American Friends Service Committee) wrote that "Workers in our Berlin Center found a new freedom in making emigration arrangements for Jewish families and in bringing relief. This short reprieve meant the difference between life and death to some families, at least."[26]

These examples illustrate a distinctive feature of Quaker activism at its best: commitment to ease suffering and promote justice without dehumanizing those who commit evil. We must know need and suffering, injustice and oppression; without that knowledge we would never bestir ourselves beyond our insulated comfort. But when obsession with evil so darkens our vision that we forget the Light and lose our way, we regress from inspiration to desperation. No longer tasting the "fruits of the Spirit," we are consumed by impotent rage. This is the path of partisan fear-mongering and heated political rhetoric, of suicide bombers and "Christian" militias; it leads ultimately to self-righteous violence and the effort to dominate others. If our efforts are to "produce God's righteousness," they must come from a place of deep renewal; in order to say "No!" with courage, we must be able to say "Yes!" with gladness. In the words of Fox's great vision, whenever we feel overcome by the "ocean of darkness," we must reawaken to the "ocean of Light"—"the infinite love of God."

Discernment

The Loving Presence does not burden us equally with all things, but considerately puts upon each of us just a few central tasks as emphatic responsibilities. For each of us, these special undertakings are our share in the joyous burden of love.

—Thomas Kelly[27]

To open ourselves to the weeping of the world requires courage; more challenging still is to decide what part each shall play in drying that ocean of tears. Contemporary media ply us with blatant examples of indignity, injustice and suffering. Because our biological evolution favored those who were alert to the rustle of a potential predator in the underbrush over those who ignored such hints of danger, we are wired to give our fullest attention to threat, and prone to prurient fascination with mayhem and abuse. This fascination is itself harmful; for example, seared upon the consciousness of all who saw them are the horrifying televised images of the collapse of the World Trade Center Twin Towers, repeatedly served up to our obsessive gaze and shaping our responses to other perceived threats.

In the face of such a barrage, persons of good will may be immobilized, retreating into cynicism or denial. Human hearts can absorb only so much trauma. Alternatively we may ratchet up our anger with each successive outrage, losing our moral footing amidst the carnage.

Regardless of our religious or ethical identity, we cannot reasonably expect to save the world single-handedly. How then shall each of us discern our own proper tasks, leaving to others what is not ours to do? In addressing the question, Friends have historically taken their cue from 1 Corinthians 12, in which St. Paul enumerated varieties of gifts, all inspired by the same Spirit. "For just as the body is one and has many members...so it is with Christ." Margaret Fell in her appeal to "Friends in the North" drew upon this image of the Body of Christ.

Discernment thus begins with accepting that one cannot do everything, nor should one try. Obsession about evils that lie beyond one's reach serves only to increase the weeping, not diminish it. Shedding excessive expectations, we must listen both to the murmurings of our hearts and to the wisdom of our spiritual friends.

This is tender ground, easily violated. We are notoriously capable of deceiving ourselves—and perhaps nowhere so readily as when we imagine that we are "following the will of God." Ancient and modern history abounds with instances of what Friends regard as false "leadings" that have led to cruelty, injustice, war and oppression. Religious wars, slavery, racism, sexism, suicide bombings, and many other evils have all been rationalized as "God's will." Thus when we sense that we are experiencing a leading of the Spirit, careful discernment is required.

In Friends' perspective, genuine leadings are characterized by love, not hate; a commitment to unify, not divide; an impulse to heal, not destroy. A genuine leading may announce itself through overheard conversation that speaks directly to one's heart[28]; it may arise as a dream, preoccupation or concern that one cannot shake off; or it may become clear through painful realization that one's beliefs and actions are not congruent. Awareness of a leading may unfold slowly over time, as one's heart opens more fully to Truth. It may be work that is begun reluctantly, yet grows into a labor of love.

There is no formula, no infallible marker by which a genuine leading may be recognized. In Quaker perspective, religious zeal is not proof of a true leading. Early Friends were quite aware of the dangers of undisciplined fervor. Quakers were often confused with the Ranters, another 17th-century religious group, who (in the words of Hugh Barbour, a leading Quaker scholar) "claimed that since they were redeemed and led by the Spirit, they could do no wrong, and so followed impulses into all kinds of immorality and anarchy."[29] To counter such anarchism, Friends insisted upon *corporate* discernment (rather than purely individual conviction) as one test of religious insight.

Often, nudges from others are required before we recognize our own leadings. In Quaker tradition, those with a gift for discerning, naming and lifting up the ministry of others were formally recognized as "elders." Whether formally recognized or not, the spiritual insight and guidance of trusted elders can be helpful in discerning and following a leading. It is also useful to consult with others whom one trusts as spiritual mentors—good listeners who are spiritually experienced and seasoned, able to hear beneath the words to the underlying motion of the Spirit.[30] Often, however, recognition of a leading arises in the privacy of one's heart, as one attempts to discern a way forward:

> *Several years ago, having just published a manuscript that had occupied me for several years, I am ready to take a break from writing and turn to other matters. Despite these plans, I find myself preoccupied with a new writing project. Even as I busy myself with other things, something originating outside my conscious agenda insinuates into the interstices of*

my life. At odd moments of the day and night, a persistent feeling overcomes me that something needs to be said—and that I am the one to say it. As I lie awake at night, or sit during my morning meditation period, or drive my car alone, insights spontaneously spring up: a point that needs to be made, a deft turn of phrase, unexpected links with other resources. I keep a pen and pad of paper handy to record these visitations, sensing that what I am putting into words may be helpful to others. Eventually I yield, committing myself to the new project.

Am I under the sway of a compulsive obsession? I have known genuine obsessions, with their undercurrent of fear. This is different. Unlike obsessive compulsive behavior, which is driven by anxiety and yields only momentary relief, when I respond to these impulses, I feel excited, liberated, joyful. Though my efforts are mentally strenuous, they have a quality of spontaneous play, as uplifting energy breaks into my life.

Had I been born into another time and place, had I been raised within another set of cultural and religious beliefs, I might give another name to the source of my inspiration. I might say that I have been visited by an angel, or by a deceased elder from another realm, or by occult signals from the stars. I might attribute my "obsession" to a personal muse or daimon. I might regard it as simply an eruption from the depths of my own unconscious. But I have been raised among Friends—and thus I turn to the language and explanation that comes most naturally to me: I tell myself that I am experiencing a "leading."[31]

Although in this instance I did not talk to others about my decision, such spiritual counsel might have helped me to recognize more quickly what I was called to do.

As Way Opens

In her superb study, *Decision Making and Spiritual Discernment*, Nancy Bieber identifies "three strands of spiritual discernment"[32]:

- **Willingness:** "An attitude of willingness is a combination of 'Help!' and 'Yes!'" We must decide to open ourselves to the wisdom and direction that is available to us. "We need to open ourselves to what is life-giving, say 'Yes' to 'what is good,' and then 'listen carefully' so that we may live."

- **Attentiveness:** "Being attentive to what is true and real is at the heart of spiritual decision making....The word *discernment* is about paying attention, about noticing those fine differences that are complicated and hard to distinguish." "Being in the now, the present, is the only way to get where we need to go."[33]

- **Responsiveness:** Willingness to open ourselves to insight and attentiveness to the reality of our lives are not enough; following a leading requires the willingness to act on the basis of the guidance that has come to us.

A distinctive marker of an authentic leading is that even when it presents grave challenges and difficulties, answering its call somehow seems natural and right—not necessarily in our rational deliberations, but within our body and heart. This rightness may be felt in each of the three strands identified by Bieber. Perhaps after a period of uncertainty and indecision, our resistance dissolves and we become willing to acknowledge the truth. A path forward emerges out of the mist—now so obvious that we wonder why we were blind to it. A friend makes an off-hand remark that (if we notice) points unambiguously to the path we are called to take. When we act upon a true leading, we often experience unexpected confirmation: difficulties evaporate, others are eased, and resources for our journey come unexpectedly to hand. A celebrated description is found in W. H. Murray's *The Scottish Himalayan Expedition*:

> Until one is committed, there is hesitancy, the chance to draw back, always ineffectiveness. Concerning all acts of initiative (and creation) there is one elementary truth the ignorance of which kills countless ideas and splendid plans: that the moment one definitely commits oneself, then providence moves too. A whole stream of events issues from the decision, raising in one's favor all manner of unforeseen incidents, meetings and material assistance, which no man (sic) could have dreamt would have come his way.[34]

Practicing willingness, attentiveness and responsiveness, we find that the world becomes less dense and more beckoning; we now move (as Friends like to say) "as way opens." Right action takes on a Taoist flavor: Taoism, "the watercourse way,"[35] counsels supple adaptability to the exigencies of the moment. Instead of pushing through a thicket of confusion, we find ourselves entering an open field of clarity and simplicity: "For God is a God not of disorder, but of peace." (I Corinthians 14:33)

Nancy Bieber observes that "Though Spirit-led decision making seems to focus on ourselves and our lives, it actually places us in truer relationship with the world around us."[36] In the end, we discover that there is no conflict between personal liberation and service to a higher good. Plumbing our own depths, we awaken to our connection with others—to what Thich Nhat Hahn calls "interbeing." Friend Lloyd Lee Wilson summarizes the intrinsic link between opening to Presence and mending the world: "It is our surrender of all to God that empowers us to stand in that place of worship and witness."[37] Finding the work to which we are called is not the calculation of an isolated self, exploring where to invest its private energies—but discovering what already lives within us, uniting us with all of creation.

CHAPTER NINE

WALKING CHEERFULLY OVER THE WORLD

Enlightenment is already here; we just need to touch it and know it and trust it.

—Pema Chodron[1]

The imperfect is our paradise.

—Wallace Stevens[2]

In the Time of Sorrow —and Joy

In the night I lie awake, distressed by difficulties facing loved ones. My efforts to put things right seem to have worsened the situation and strained my relationships with those involved. Hours earlier, my wife had said, "You can't do anything about it." Still I struggle fruitlessly in my mind.

At last I arise in the darkness to sit upon my

*meditation cushion. Settling into zazen, I feel the famil-
iar kinesthetic and visceral sensations: my shoulders
uncurl and drop freely from my spine; my chest opens,
lifting pressure from my lungs and heart; my belly re-
leases and drops. I direct my attention to the emotional distress itself—the flailing thoughts tinged with desperation, fantasies building to a silent crescendo of
imagined catastrophe.*

*Suspending willfulness, I give myself over to dis-
passionate inspection of my emotional turmoil. Space
opens up. The cords of clinging loosen; the knot un-
tangles. That which had troubled me remains unresolved, and the pain that it engenders has not disap-
peared—yet my relationship to that pain has shifted.
No longer straining to escape the distress by manipu-
lating the conditions that give rise to it, I open to the
distress and allow it to rest in my heart. As the mists
of my confusion lift, I reawaken to what has always
been present to me—a boundless field of compassion.
No longer struggling to excise the hurt, I make room
for it within my heart and surrender my brokenness
into adoration of love. Resting in peace, I return to my
bed and sleep.*

In my own experience, sorrow and joy are inextricably en-
twined; when fully faced, bitterness can give birth to delight.
"Crushing truths perish from being acknowledged," writes Albert
Camus.[3] Rumi says that the secret to living an abundant life is
"To find joy in the heart when the time of sorrow comes."[4] No
ephemeral pleasure, such joy is an assurance that sustains one
in the presence of pain. Judeo-Christian scripture offers countless examples of this reassuring truth, couched in theistic language: "Those of steadfast mind you keep in peace—in peace
because they trust in you," declares Isaiah (26:3). "Even though
I walk through the darkest valley, I fear no evil; for you are with

me; your rod and your staff—they comfort me," writes the Psalmist (23:4).

Our most beloved stories of spiritual renewal do not depict a smooth and easy path to redemption. Hearing promises of easy grace, our "bullshit detector" sounds the alarm. Even as we indulge in wishful thinking, a rigorously honest corner of our mind is skeptical. At some level, we know that "Life is not like that."

In 1943, Eva Hermann, a German Quaker, was found guilty by Nazi authorities of offering support and protection to Jews in her neighborhood. She was incarcerated in Mannheim (her husband was imprisoned elsewhere) and not released until 1945 when the area was liberated by American troops. Pressed to write an account of these traumatic years, Hermann responded with vibrant testimony to the power of faith and compassion. She begins her account with this startling admission: "It may seem paradoxical for me to say that I would not have missed the experiences of these two years of my life in a Nazi prison for anything. But it is so."[5] Cut off from family and friends, deprived of freedom and comfort, confined within a cold castle that was regularly struck by artillery, Eva Hermann nevertheless found strength in the commitment of the prisoners to compassionate care for one another. She quotes a Greek physician who, after losing everything to war in the Balkans, gave himself to tireless aid to others: "What is left but love and service?" In the stark cruelty of the prison, simple acts of kindness became heroic.

Before her imprisonment, Hermann had met Thomas Kelly, the American Quaker mystic and scholar. She writes, "At the time he was a vexation and a stumbling block to me. We were... drowning in a sea of sorrow and trouble which was engulfing our Jewish friends, without being able to help them. And Thomas Kelly spoke to us of joy. It seemed so cheap to come out of secure America and talk about joy. I rejected his message, and yet knew in my inmost heart that I was not being just to him... ." Her full recognition of Kelly's luminous insight came some eight years later, as she suffered her own travail in prison: "We political prisoners did not suppose that we would be allowed to survive the end of the Third Empire; we believed that destruction was before us. And I dwelt in the very joy which I had failed to understand in Thomas Kelly."

Eva Hermann survived. So many whom she had struggled to help did not. Yet faith also flourished within the horror of the death camps themselves. In his classic study, *Man's Search for Meaning*, Viktor Frankl reports that despite the degrading conditions of life in Auschwitz, "The religious interest of the prisoners... was the most sincere imaginable. The depth and vigor of religious belief often surprised and moved a new arrival. Most impressive in this connection were improvised prayers or services in the corner of a hut, or in the darkness of a locked cattle truck in which we were brought back from a distant worksite, tired, hungry, and frozen in our ragged clothing."[6]

The lessons that Eva Hermann drew from her incarceration mirror those drawn by Frankl himself. He writes, "For the first time in my life I saw the truth as it is set into song by so many poets, proclaimed as the final wisdom by so many thinkers. The truth—that love is the ultimate and the highest goal to which (one) can aspire. Then I grasped the meaning of the greatest secret that human poetry and human thought and belief have to impart: *The salvation of (humankind) is through love and in love.*"[7]

Responding to Suffering

These insights were expressed through acts of kindness carried out within the belly of implacable evil. Frankl writes that the prisoners' redemption came not by overcoming their Nazi captors, but through an inner decision to respond affirmatively to their suffering. "Suffering had become a task on which we did not want to turn our backs. We had realized its hidden

opportunities for achievement"; "it is just such an exceptional-
ly difficult external situation which gives (us) the opportunity to
grow spiritually beyond (ourselves)."[8]

The multiple imprisonments of George Fox, Margaret Fell,
Isaac Penington, William Penn, and other early Friends illustrate
this theme: that genuine spiritual growth comes not from finding
ways to avoid the difficult challenges of life, but from meeting
and living through those challenges with honesty, courage, and
humility. As we do this, we find untapped spiritual resources—
and way opens to a deeper affirmation of life and love.

This is a central message not only of Christianity but of other
great religions as well. But is religion the sole provenance of all
such inspiring accounts? Must we first declare allegiance to the
supernatural (as described by one or another body of religious
doctrine) before we will be granted the sustenance that our souls
require in times of trial?

I believe that the answer to both of these questions is no.
Those who are able "to find joy in the heart when the time of
sorrow comes" indeed often cite religious teachings to explain
their solace. In difficult times, many are sustained by reminding themselves of the spiritual promises they have received. Yet
even without invoking religious claims, the sheer courage to face
and bear up under the suffering of life can yield sustaining truth.
Writing at the outset of World War II, as his world was crumbling
under the onslaught of the Nazis, Albert Camus wrote, "I don't
know whether this world has a meaning that transcends it. But I
know that I do not know that meaning and that it is impossible
for me just now to know it."[9] A modest, courageous man who
was active in the underground French resistance, Camus wrote
of the joys that sprang up unbidden in the midst of his seemingly hopeless struggle to live a life of integrity: "The absurd man
says yes and his effort will henceforth be unceasing.... Sisyphus teaches the higher fidelity that negates the gods and raises
rocks. He too concludes that all is well.... The struggle toward

the heights is enough to fill a man's heart. One must imagine Sisyphus happy."[10]

In my course on human happiness, "Theories of the Good Life," I assign a midterm paper on the topic, "One Year to Live." In this assignment I ask my students to imagine they will certainly die in twelve months, and to describe how they would spend their remaining time, first if they were to follow the teachings of the authors we have studied in the course, and then what they would actually do. As the deadline[11] for the paper approaches, the class meets outside on a sunny spring morning. Rosettes of students sit on the lawn, discussing the topic for the day. As I move from one small group to another, a young man approaches, eyeing me intently. He is tall and wan, with a large bald spot on the front of his scalp. He looks vaguely familiar. Extending a limp hand, he introduces himself: he is a graduate who took my class, completing the very assignment that my students now face. Soon after graduation he was diagnosed with terminal cancer of the lungs and esophagus. Having undergone a regimen of an experimental chemotherapy drug, he is in brief remission—and on hospice.

I am shocked by his story, yet grateful that he has approached me. I ask him whether he would be willing to talk with my current students, who are preparing to write on what is for them a hypothetical scenario that he is actually living through. He agrees. We meet later that week. His wife (who married him shortly after he was diagnosed) is present, along with some 25 of my students. We listen with rapt attention as he talks—of being so wretchedly ill from the chemo that he vomited repeatedly for days; of losing his senses of taste and smell; of being so weak that he had to crawl on hands and knees to the bathroom. All is stated without pathos or melodrama. He also describes his joy at being a part of a small community of other cancer patients who support one another in their travails.

I ask him if he holds out hope of ultimate recovery in order to sustain his spirits. His "no" is emphatic; attachment to such a hope would be emotionally disastrous. Then with transparent sincerity that dispels all possible doubt, he says that if he were magically given a choice to remain in his present life (with its physical distress and brief prospects) or return to the conventional existence he would probably have led had he not contracted cancer, he would choose his present life. "Why?" Because the beauty that he now experiences, the fullness of heart-to-heart intimacy, the mutual love and support, is so precious and so far beyond what he had anticipated before he became ill, that he could not bear to give it up.

As we part, I am filled with heartbroken wonder and gratitude. I never see my former student again. Six months later his wife calls to tell me he has passed away. Early in the new year, she and I, together with two of his closest hospice friends, drive into the local mountains to deposit his ashes at the edge of a stream near one of his favorite hiking trails, and to remember his life—a testimonial to the truth of Viktor Frankl's words, that salvation "is through love and in love."

Love Beyond the Small Self

We may not require metaphysical hypotheses to face the challenging difficulties of our lives—but we do need to remember that we are not alone; we are part of something precious that is greater than ourselves. Humans find this "something greater" in many places, some modest and largely healthy, others decidedly pathological. Commitments to family, friends, community, and larger social groupings can be rich sources of meaning. Yet destructive ideologies such as Stalinism and fascism have also traded on submersion of the individual into a larger entity that supposedly gives purpose to life. The power of ideology to inspire sacrificial devotion to dreadful destruction has been thoroughly documented by human history.

By what criterion may we distinguish healthy from unhealthy, life-affirming from life-denying forms of self-transcendence? I find such a criterion in a familiar place: the spiritual message of loving kindness that is found throughout the world's great wisdom traditions, including Buddhism, Judaism, and Christianity. A favorite Buddhist text of His Holiness the 14th Dalai Lama (who has often said simply, "My religion is kindness") is the "Bodhisattva's Vow":

> May all beings everywhere plagued by sufferings of
> body and mind, obtain an ocean of happiness and joy… .
> May no living creature suffer, commit evil or ever fall ill.
> May no one be afraid or belittled, with a mind weighted
> down by depression… . May those whose bodies are worn
> with toil, be restored on finding repose. May the naked find
> clothing, the hungry find food. May the thirsty find water… .
> May the poor find wealth, those weak with sorrow find joy;
> may the hopeless find hope, constant happiness and pros-
> perity. … May all who are sick and ill quickly be freed from
> their ailments… . May the frightened cease to be afraid and
> those bound be freed. May the powerless find power and
> the people think of benefiting each other. For as long as
> space remains, for as long as sentient beings remain, until
> then may I too remain to dispel the miseries of the world.[12]

The centrality of loving kindness in a spiritual life is affirmed by the contemporary Buddhist teacher, Jack Kornfield:

> In undertaking a spiritual life, what matters is simple:
> *We must make certain that our path is connected with*

our heart... . The things that matter most in our lives are not fantastic or grand. They are the moments when we touch one another, when we are there in the most attentive or caring way... . Mother Teresa put it like this: "In this life we cannot do great things. We can only do small things with great love."... All other spiritual teachings are in vain if we cannot love. Even the most exalted states and the most exceptional spiritual accomplishments are unimportant if we cannot be happy in the most basic and ordinary ways, if, with our hearts, we cannot touch one another and the life we have been given. What matters is how we live.[13]

Familiar passages in Judeo-Christian-Islamic Scripture echo this theme:

> You shall love your neighbor as yourself.
>
> —Leviticus 19:18

> I give you a new commandment, that you will love one another. Just as I have loved you, you also should love one another. By this everyone will know that you are my disciples, if you have love for one another.
>
> —John 13: 34-35

> God is love, and those who abide in love abide in God and God abides in them... . There is no fear in love, but perfect love casts out fear.
>
> —I John 4:16-18

Quaker writings endorse the Christian message:

> And all Friends, take heed of jars and strife, for that... will eat out the seed in you... . Therefore dwell in Love and Life and in the Power and Seed of God, which is the honorable, royal state... . See that you are in the Life... which will edify the body, and not in a brittle, peevish, hasty, fretful mind... that Love may continue in the body, that the Seed may spread over all, that unity may be kept.
>
> –George Fox[14]

Our life is love, and peace, and tenderness; and bearing one with another, and forgiving one another, and not laying accusations one against another; but praying one for another, and helping one another up with a tender hand.

—Isaac Penington[15]

Care of self is inseparable from care for others and for all of creation. Yet without dedicated spiritual practice, I cannot keep this truth present to my heart. Implanted in me are egoistic compulsions that draw me away from the bond between myself and others.[16] With spiritual practice, however, I find my life rounding into a deeper vision of wholeness, of what Christians traditionally have called "the Body of Christ." As boundaries soften between myself and others, openness converges upon compassion. Even as I feel more keenly the tears of the world, my distress is transformed within an enveloping joy.

The Kingdom of Heaven Is Now

The kingdom of God is not food and drink but righteousness and peace and joy in the Holy Spirit.

—Romans 14:17

No heaven can come to us unless our hearts find rest in it today. Take heaven! No peace lies in the future which is not hidden in this present little instant. Take peace! The gloom of the world is but a shadow. Behind it, yet within our reach, is joy. There is radiance and glory in darkness, could we but see. And to see, we have only to look. I beseech you to look! Life is so generous a giver. But we, judging its gifts by their covering, cast them away as ugly or heavy or hard. Remove the covering, and you will find beneath it a living splendor, woven of love by wisdom, with power. Welcome it, grasp it, and you touch the angel's hand that brings it to you. Everything we call a trial, a sorrow or a duty, believe me, that angel's hand is there. The gift is there and the wonder of an overshadowing presence. Your joys, too, be not content with them as joys. They, too, conceal diviner gifts. Life is so full of meaning and purpose, so full of beauty beneath its covering, that you will find earth but cloaks your heaven. Courage then to claim it.

—Fra Giovanni Giocondo[17]

Shall I imagine a perfect place beyond space and time, where all weeping has ceased and joy is unending? Shall I hang my hopes on such a world, regarding life on this earth as a poor imitation? Shall I imagine myself to be among a privileged "elect" who have tickets to that perfect world and look with concern or pity upon those who will be "left behind"?

Humility requires me to say that I do not know of a perfect world. Indeed, I do not truly understand the nature of my own consciousness, much less its destiny. Lacking any personal experience that would clarify this mystery, I suspend judgment and remain agnostic. I neither affirm nor deny another reality, and decline to pattern my life after such a supposition, while remaining open to its possible truth.[18] The word "humility" springs from the same etymological root as "humus," naming the organic constituents of the soil.[19] Both words invite me to attend to what I know—the imperfect, fecund earth in all of its shifting flux and wonder.

Belief that bliss is found only in a remote afterlife, accessible to a few and presided over by a harsh and judging deity, appears to be a late development in Christian theology. Early Christian images locate paradise in this world, either as a definite (although vaguely specified) place on earth, or as the condition of everyday life itself, infused by Living Spirit. In their revolutionary study, *Saving Paradise: How Christianity Traded Love of This World for Crucifixion and Empire*, Rita Nakashima Brock and Rebecca Ann Parker write that in the early centuries of Christianity, "paradise... was this world, permeated and blessed by the Spirit of God. It was on the earth." "Paradise was described in terms recognized as earthly life at its best.... . It could be experienced as real—not as a permanent state of being, but as aspects of life itself."[20]

Early Friends affirmed this realized eschatology: while the fullness of the Kingdom of God[21] unfolds over time, that Reality is even now within and among us. What must we do to allow ourselves to become aware of Presence? Through pure passion we surrender ourselves wholly to the reality of our lives and "stand all naked and bare before the Lord." Early Friends called this "taking up one's cross" or "standing in the cross." Through this utter surrender, we are freed from the burden of sinfulness and are liberated. Describing the theological views of 17th-century Friends, Quaker scholar Gerard Guiton summarizes:

> For the Kingdom to be present and "at hand," Jesus added another important factor—personal transformation (metanoia)—a reality that is possible only with God's help. It involves repentance in the sense of giving up one's own agenda (and fears and ego) and trusting completely in God. ...Transformation results from *kenosis*, an "emptying" of one's self-originated understanding and one's "convincement" of the truth.[22]

> The Kingdom incorporated the dynamic strength of God's Life and Power translated into the daily routine of the individual as if (this Life and Power) were one with his or her consciousness.... . (Early Friends') intimacy with the Kingdom took shape through worship based on silence and holy obedience, on their suffering and works of justice, peace and mercy. In this way, their Kingdom lives were made tangible.... . The compassion, hope and wholeness that were of the Kingdom could never, therefore, be abstractions emanating from a remote Other.... . The "now" factor differentiated the Quakers from the Calvinists and rationalists who were convinced their faith and practice would be enriched only with the physical Second Coming.[23]

God was present *now* to all people, the "Day" was *now*," the Word incarnate *now* among those who lived in Truth.[24]

In very different cultural clothing, Buddhist accounts of enlightenment experiences echo this theme. Jack Kornfield affirms the ever-present reality of the enlightened state:

Zen master Dogen, the founder of Soto Zen in Japan, declared, "To be enlightened is to be intimate with all things." The air we breathe, the wind that blows around us, the earth that we walk upon, the lives of others around us, the most intimate things of our lives, are the place of our sleep or of our awakening... . Only in the intimacy of the timeless present can we awaken. This intimacy connects us to one another, allows us to belong, and in this belonging, we experience love. In this we move beyond our separateness, our contraction, our limited sense of ourselves... . Awakening is not far away; it is nearer than near... .

Our capacity for intimacy is built on deep respect, a presence that allows what is true to express itself, to be discovered. Intimacy can arise in any moment; it is an act of surrender, a gift that excludes nothing... . When we become intimate with all things, we discover rest, well-being, and wholeness in this very body. We recognize that we, and all life around us, are supposed to be here, that we belong here as much as the trees and the sun and the turning earth. There comes a healing, an opening, and a grace. The harmony of all things arises for us like the wisdom of Dame Julian of Norwich, who so beautifully declared, "all shall be well and all manner of things shall be well." In intimacy we discover a profound sense of belonging and wholeness that allows us to touch all that we encounter.[25]

Ruben Habito, a Jesuit and "the first Catholic whose experience of enlightenment was authenticated by recognized Zen masters," credits his "explosive experience" of *kensho* with giving him full appreciation of the Christian teaching "of an ever-present wonderment with every breath, every step, every smile... every leaf, every flower, every raindrop, realized as literally *nothing* but the grace-filled gift from the infinite and ever-flowing divine love!"[26]

A Simple Sense of Delight

Surrendering into this moment, I am embraced by the fullness of life—tears and joy, labor and repose, despair and exaltation. No longer straining to be elsewhere, I reconcile with the present. If hell is hatred of being, heaven is surely gladness of being. Revealed in its splendor, life becomes playful activity, an overflowing of joy and good will.

The Gospel of Matthew closes with these reassuring words: "Lo, I am with you always, even unto the end of the world." (28:20, KJV) Jesus is not offering a "rain check" that can be fulfilled only in another life. Rather, he declares that redemptive love is a constant *present* reality, even in the darkest, most horrific moments imaginable. Shrinking back from the challenges of life assures only that we live in fragile fear. In contrast, giving ourselves fully to the moment with all of the trust and good will that we can muster opens us to unexpected healing possibilities. "Live up to the Light thou hast, and more will be granted thee," writes the 19th-century Quaker Caroline Fox.[27]

A classic Christian account of this surrender is St. Paul's declaration: "I have been crucified with Christ, and it is no longer I who live, but it is Christ who lives in me." (Galatians 2:19-20) Yet such surrender is not confined to Christian teachings, but is found wherever we give ourselves wholeheartedly to the reality of love. Interpreting Jesus' promise, the Sufi mystic, Rumi, writes, "'Lo, I am with you always' means when you look for God, God is in the look of your eyes, in the thought of looking, nearer to you than your self, or things that have happened to you. There's no need to go outside."[28]

Sakyong Mipham Rinpoche, the son and spiritual successor of the Tibetan Buddhist teacher, Chogyam Trungpa Rinpoche, tells the story of a Tibetan Lama who was visiting America for the first time. He was asked, "Who seems happier—the nomads in Tibet or the people you have met in America?" Upon reflection, "he had no doubt that the simple nomads of Tibet are happier and more cheerful.... Simplicity allows us to experience our mind in a raw and naked state..., one of the most welcome and important aspects of practicing and studying Buddhist teachings is that we begin to trust our mind and discover the inherent goodness in it. The result is feeling cheerful."[29] Space opens within the mind when we practice disciplined Buddhist meditation or its Quaker counterpart, "standing still in the Light." "When there's space in the mind, the mind relaxes and we feel a simple sense of delight," writes Sakyong Mipham. This delight exists in the midst of awareness of life's difficulties: "Contemplating the truth of pain and suffering does not lead to depression. Rather, it helps us to appreciate what we have, which is Buddha-nature.... Knowing that we are all naturally awake brings delight. ... (T)he day does not have to be sunny for us to be cheerful."[30] In a similar vein, another Buddhist teacher, Sylvia Boorstein, teaches that "Heaven can be right here on earth, when we live with friendliness, compassion, joy, and equanimity."[31]

The natural condition of such a life is cheerfulness. Writing from yet another prison, in Launceston in 1656, in perhaps the best known of his many pastoral epistles, George Fox charged Friends with the following:

> And this is the word of the Lord God to you all, and a charge to you all in the presence of the living God, be patterns, be examples in all countries, places, islands, nations, wherever you come; that your carriage and life may preach among all sorts of people, and to them. Then you will come to walk cheerfully over the world, answering that

of God in every one; whereby in them ye may be a blessing, and make the witness of God in them to bless you. Then to the lord God you will be a sweet savour and a blessing.[32]

The prisons of this world—Mannheim, Buchenwald, Lubanka, Launceston, and countless others, past and present—are massive monuments to fear, tangible testimonies of hatred. They remind us of the incomprehensible cruelty and injustice that we inflict upon one another. They are also metaphors for the human condition when it is locked into spiritual darkness. Yet Eva Hermann, Viktor Frankl, Walter Ciszek, and George Fox also demonstrate that the Light which enlightens everyone dawns even in such earthly hells—provided that we extend ourselves through acts of human kindness, generosity, and love.

Spiritual practice is not a search for something that is absent from our lives. Rather, it is the discipline of reawakening to a Reality that is forever infused within us—a Sacred Source in which even now, *in this very moment*, we "live and move and have our being." Because we are eternally enfolded within this Source, to live into the present is to know that Source immediately and intimately. It is to taste a quietude so profound, a reassurance so expansive, that all of creation is embraced within it. From such wholeness flows a river of justice, healing, and love. Outward action is no longer heedless of inward solace, but unites with it in grace and delight. Our fears soften, hearts open—and we find that indeed, our yoke is easy, our burden is light. As we go about our small part in the urgent business of mending a broken world, we find that we are—here, now, and always—basking in the womb of God.

ENDNOTES

INTRODUCTION

1. Karen Armstrong, *The Case for God* (New York: Knopf, 2009), p. xiii.

2. Ibid.

3. Ibid., p. xv.

4. Although the importance of practical wisdom is emphasized in Aristotle's *Nichomachean Ethics* (see Book VI, Chapters 5, 12, 13), courses in ethical theory and classical philosophy typically note this insight—only to put aside its cultivation in order to explore theoretical puzzles.

5. See Heinrich Dumoulin, S.J., *A History of Zen Buddhism* (Boston: Beacon Press, 1963), p. 67. Dumoulin dates Bodhidharma's life to the early 5th Century C.E. and attributes these four lines to a Zen master from the Tang era, Nan-chuan Pu-yan (748-834). See Dumoulin, Chapter 5, ftnt. 1.

6. *Shobogenzo*; quoted by Jack Kornfield, *A Path with Heart: A Guide Through the Perils and Promises of Spiritual Life* (New York: Bantam,1993), pp. 332-339.

7. *Journal of George Fox*, ed. by John L. Nickalls (London: Religious Society of Friends, 1975), p. 33.

8. Ibid., p. 27.

9. Ibid., p. 33.

10. Dumoulin, p. 68.

11. *Journal*, p. 45. Fox refers to Acts 7:48: "The Most High dwelleth not in temples made with hands."

12. "Introduction" by Geoffrey F. Nuttall, DD., to Fox, *Journal*, p. xxxiii.

13. *Journal*, p. 9f.

14. "Extracts from William Penn's Preface," in Fox, *Journal*, p. xliii.

15. Published in 1696. Available without charge online.

16. Sandokai, in Wikipedia, accessed on 23 August 2012.

17. A traditional tool of Zen masters is a gnarled stick sometimes used in personal interviews to strike their students unexpectedly, in an effort to wake them abruptly into the moment.

18. *Knowing the Mystery of Life Within: Selected Writings of Isaac Penington in their Historical and Theological Context*, selected and introduced by R. Melvin Keiser and Rosemary Moore (London: Quaker Books, 2005), front matter epigraph.

19. Alfred North Whitehead, *Science and the Modern World* (New York: Free Press, 1925, 1997), p. 51.

20. Many editions. *This from Lao Tzu: Text, Notes, and Comments, by ChenKu-ying*, translated and adapted by Rhett Y. W. Young and Roger T. Ames (San Francisco: Chinese Materials Center, Inc., 1977), p. 51.

21. Paul F. Knitter, *Without Buddha I Could Not Be a Christian* (Oxford: Oneworld Publications, 2009), p. 65. Knitter is Paul Tillich Professor of Theology, World Religions and Culture at Union Theological Seminary.

22. Jack Kornfield, *After the Ecstasy, the Laundry: How the Heart Grows Wise on the Spiritual Path* (New York: Bantam, 2000), pp. 218f.

23. "Questions Which Tend not to Edification, Sermon Number 1," from *The Lesser Malunkyaputta Sutra*, Translated from the Maijhima-Nikaya.

24. "The Testimony of Margaret Fox Concerning her Late Husband George Fox," in *Hidden In Plain Sight: Quaker Women's Writings 1650-1700*, ed. by Mary Garman, et. al. (Wallingford, PA: Pendle Hill Publications, 1996), p. 235.

25. *The Maxims of Marcel Proust*, ed. by Justin O'Brien (New York: Columbia University Press, 1948), p. 181.

26. I have discovered that my outlook falls roughly into the category of "apophatic theology." This longstanding tradition has its roots in "negative theology" *(via negativa)*—the outlook that no positive description is adequate to name or express the reality of the Divine Good. "Negative theology... is often allied with mysticism, which focuses on a spontaneous or cultivated individual experience of the

divine reality beyond the realm of ordinary perception, an experience often unmediated by the structures of traditional organized religion or the conditioned role-playing and learned defensive behavior of the outer man.... The Divine is ineffable... it eludes definition by definition." (From *Apophatic Theology* in Wikipedia, accessed on 23 July 2012.) Both Zen and the mystical aspects of Quakerism exemplify this outlook.

27. Fox, *Journal*, p. 263.

28. Ibid., p. 28.

29. This phrase comes from Thich Nhat Hanh, a Vietnamese Zen Buddhist master who has done much to popularize Zen in mainstream Western religious thought.

30. Preface to *Lyrical Ballads*, Second Edition (1800).

31. Final lines of "Conclusion." Many editions.

Part I: PURGATION

CHAPTER ONE:

A QUAKER IN THE ZENDO

1. The reading list included Leo Tolstoy's *The Death of Ivan Ilych*, Hermann Hesse's *Siddhartha*, Victor Frankl's *Man's Search for Meaning*, and Mitch Albom's *Tuesdays with Morris*, as well as an anthology published in 1983, *Ways of Wisdom: Readings on the Good Life*, edited by Steve Smith (Lanham, MD: University Press of America), with selections from some 40 authors, including Nietzsche, Kafka, Plato, Epicurus, Epictetus, Shankara, Freud, Rogers, Thoreau, the Bible, Camus, Suzuki, Watts, and others.

2. Particularly influential were Paramahansa Yogananda's *The Autobiography of a Yogi* (Los Angeles: Self-Realization Fellowship, 1946, 1972), and the writings of Alan Watts, D.T. Suzuki, and Nancy Wilson Ross.

3. Three books eventually were published: *Everyday Zen: Love and Work* (1989); *Nothing Special: Living Zen* (1993); and *Now Zen* (1995), all by Charlotte Joko Beck with Steve Smith (San Francisco: HarperSanFrancisco). *Now Zen* consists of excerpts from the two previous books, in a smaller format.

4. Robert Kennedy, *Zen Spirit, Christian Spirit: The Place of Zen in Christian Life* (New York: Continuum, 1995, 2001), p. 14.

5. Kennedy, *Zen Spirit*, p. 17.

6. William James, *The Varieties of Religious Experience: A Study in Human Nature* (New York: Mentor, 1958), p. 78f.

7. Harold Kasimow, John P. Keenan, and Linda Klepinger Keenan, eds., *Beside Still Waters: Jews, Christians, and the Way of the Buddha* (Boston: Wisdom Publications, 2003), p. 90.

CHAPTER TWO:

STANDING STILL IN THE LIGHT

1. *The Journal of George Fox*, ed. by John L. Nickalls (London: Religious Society of Friends, 1975), pp. 346-348.

2. "This observing Self is usually called the Self with a capital S, or the Witness, or pure Presence, or pure Awareness, or Consciousness as such, and this Self as transparent Witness is a direct ray of the living Divine. The ultimate "I AM" is Christ, is Buddha, is Emptiness itself: such is the startling testimony of the world's great mystics and sages... " Ken Wilbur, A Brief History of Everything, Chap. 12, pp. 197-199. See the following chapter, "Pure Passion," for a fuller exploration of this process.

3. "Some Directions to the Panting Soul," in Works (Glenside, Penn.: Quaker Heritage, 1994), Vol. 2, p. 205.

4. *The Journal of George Fox*, p. 11.

5. *The Covenant Crucified: Quakers and the Rise of Capitalism* (Wallingford, PA: Pendle Hill Publications, 1995), p. 373.

6. ibid.; see esp. pp. 102-106.

7. Douglas Gwyn, *Seekers Found: Atonement in Early Quaker Experience* (Wallingford, PA: Pendle Hill Publications, 2000), p. 249.

8. *The Covenant Crucified*, p. 105.

9. Rex Ambler, *Truth of the Heart: An Anthology of George Fox* (London: Quaker Books, 2001). See especially Ambler's Preface and the concluding interpretive essay, "Making Sense of Fox." I encourage interested readers to familiarize themselves with his work.

10. *Truth of the Heart*, pp. vii-viii.

11. *Seekers Found*, p. 239.

12. George Fox, Epistle #10, 1652, in "The Power of the Lord Is Over All": *The Pastoral Letters of George Fox*, Introduced and edited by T. Canby Jones (Richmond, IN: Friends United Press, 1989), p. 7.

13. Douglas Gwyn, *Unmasking the Idols: A Journey Among Friends* (Richmond, IN: Friends United Press, 1989), p. 20.

14. *The Covenant Crucified*, p. 122.

15. Caroline Jones, "The Value of Stillness," in *Friends Journal*, April 2001 (Vol. 47, No. 4), p. 5

16. *George Fox, Epistle XLV from Works* (Philadelphia and New York: Gould and Hopper, 1831), p. 56.

17. Hugh Barbour, *The Quakers in Puritan England* (New Haven and London: Yale University Press, 1964), p. 99.

18. John Punshon, *Encounter With Silence: Reflections from the Quaker Tradition* (Richmond, IN: Friends United Press, 1987), p. 8.

19. In his writing and preaching, Fox frequently used some version of this phrase. See for example *Journal*, p. 20.

20. Paul Anderson, "Is There a Quaker Hermeneutic?" in *Quaker Religious Thought* #97 (Vol. 30, No. 3), p. 6.

21. *A Description of the Qualifications Necessary to a Gospel Minister* (Philadelphia: Pendle Hill Publications and Tract Association of Friends, 1989), p. 83f. Emphasis in original.

22. *The Quakers in Puritan England*, p. 98.

23. Epistle #95, 1655, quoted by Howard Brinton, *Friends for 300 Years: The history and beliefs of the Society of Friends since George Fox started the Quaker movement* (Wallingford, PA: Pendle Hill Publications, 1952), p. 27.

24. *Journal*, pp. 347f.

25. Mary Garman, Judith Applegate, Margaret Benefiel, Dorothy Meredith, eds., *Hidden in Plain Sight: Quaker Women's Writings 1656–1700* (Wallingford, PA: Pendle Hill Publications, 1996), p. 471.

26. Epistle #95 (1655), excerpted in *The Power of the Lord Is Over All: The Pastoral Letters of George Fox*, Introduced and edited by T. Canby Jones Richmond, IN: Friends United Press, 1989), p. 78.

27. George Fox, Epistle #11, 1652, in Jones, p. 8.

28. *Encounter With Silence*, p. 11.

29. Margaret Fell, Works, pp. 95, 136. Quoted in Barbour, *The Quakers in Puritan England*, p. 98.

30. Howard H. Brinton, *Friends for 300 Years: The history and beliefs of the Society of Friends since George Fox started the Quaker Movement* (Wallingford, PA: Pendle Hill Publications, 1952, 1965), p. 55. See Brother Lawrence, *The Practice of the Presence of God* (Old Tappan, New Jersey: Spire Books, 1958).

31. *Journal*, p. 28.

32. William Penn's Preface to *The Journal of George Fox*, op. cit., p. xliv.

33. Quoted by John Punshon, *Encounter With Silence*, p. 5.

34. "To All That Would Know the Way to the Kingdom," in Works, Vol. 4 (New York: AMS Press, 1975), p. 25.

35. Quoted in Brinton, *Friends for 300 Years*, pp. 65-66. I am indebted to Aimee Elsbree for calling my attention to this passage.

36. *Journal*, p. 79.

CHAPTER THREE:
PURE PASSION

1. *Everyday Zen: Love and Work* (New York: HarperOne, 1989), p. 108.

2. Lin Yutang, *The Importance of Living* (New York: The John Day Co., 1937). Excerpts reprinted in Steve Smith, ed., *Ways of Wisdom: Readings on the Good Life* (Lanham, MD: University Press of America, 1983). See p. 57.

3. In the early years of my recovery process, I relied primarily upon psychotherapy (and later, upon spiritual practice) rather than Alcoholics Anonymous. Yet I have great respect for 12-step programs. Veterans of such programs will notice parallels between them and my approach here.

4. Quoted in Anselm Gruen, *Heaven Begins Within You: Wisdom from the Desert Fathers* (New York: Crossroad, 2011), p. 18.

5. For a description of the class (including the reading list) see Chapter One, p. 21, footnote 1.

6. Students used a version of the Myers Briggs Temperament Inventory developed by David Keirsey, *Please Understand Me II: Temperament, Character, Intelligence* (Del Mar, CA: Prometheus, 1998).

7. Arnold Beisser, "The Paradoxical Theory of Change," in Joen Fagen & Irma Lee Shepherd, *Gestalt Therapy Now* (Palo Alto, CA: Science and Behavior Books, 1970), pp. 77-80.

8. Pema Chodron, ed. by Sandy Boucher, *Taking the Leap: Freeing Ourselves from Old Habits and Fears* (Boston & London: Shambhala, 2010), pp. 40f. Chodron teaches in the Tibetan Buddhist tradition.

9. See Chogyam Trungpa, *Cutting Through Spiritual Materialism* (Boulder, CO: Shambhala 1973).

10. Barry Magid, *Ending the Pursuit of Happiness: A Zen Guide* (Boston: Wisdom Publications, 2008), p. 10. Magid is one of Joko Beck's senior students.

11. Jon Kabat-Zinn, *Coming to Our Senses: Healing Ourselves and the World Through Mindfulness* (New York: Hyperion, 2005), pp. 61f. Kabat-Zinn is the author of the best-selling titles, *Full Catastrophe Living* (New York: Delta, 1990) and *Wherever You Go, There You Are* (New York: Hyperion, 1994), and the originator of "Mindfulness Based Stress Reduction" (MBSR), an 8-10 week structured program of complementary medicine that has gained widespread recognition for its benefits.

12. Ibid.

13. "To All That Would Know the Way to the Kingdom" (1653) in *The Works of George Fox Vol. IV*, p. 17; Epistle #11 (1652) in Jones, p. 8. See Chapter Two for a fuller description.

14. Marc Ian Barasch, *Field Notes on the Compassionate Life: A Search for the Soul of Kindness* (Rodale, 2005), p. 14.

15. Foreword to Margaret Chatterjee, *Gandhi's Religious Thought* (Notre Dame, IN: University of Notre Dame Press, 1983), p. ix.

16. *The Varieties of Religious Experience* with a Foreword by Jacques Barzun (New York: Mentor, 1958, 1961), p. 228f.

17. Blake, opening lines of "Auguries of Innocence" in *The Pickering Manuscript*.

18. *Living Zen, Loving God* (Boston: Wisdom Publications, 2004), pp. X, 6, 10.

19. Fr. Thomas Keating, "Seekers of Ultimate Mystery" (Contemplative Outreach newsletter, online June 2010).

20. *Essays in Zen Buddhism, Second Series* (London: Luzak and Company, 1933), p. 260.

21. "Metanoia" in Wikipedia, 1 March 2012.

22. *Zen Master AMA Samy, Zen Ancient & Modern: The Way to Heart Mind* (Dingigul, India: Vaigarai publications, 2010), pp. 63-66.

23. Ibid pp. 66f.

24. Thus in the *King James Version of the Bible*, when Jesus says, "suffer the little children to come unto me . . ." (Mark 10:14), this passage is rendered in the New Revised Standard Version of the Bible as "Let the little children come to me."

25. "Being Practically Spiritual: Margaret Fell and John Woolman on Integrating the Inward and Outward Life" in Western Friend, September/October 2011, p. 19.

26. In the early 19th Century, Friends found this capacity for discernment among Native Americans, observing that "the Pagans believed ... in the guidance of the Spirit." Howard Brinton, *Friends for 350 Years*, with historical update and page and line notes by Margaret Hope Bacon (Wallingford, PA: Pendle Hill Publications, 2002), p.47.

27. Emphasis added. For a provocative comparison, consider the declaration attributed to Louis XIV of France, "L'Etat, c'est moi."... "I am the state." In these (probably apocryphal) words, Louis XIV identified himself with a larger, impersonal entity. Yet he also declared, "Je m'en vais, mais l'État demeurera toujours."... "I am going away, but the State will always remain." The first declaration reflects a grandiosity that we would prefer not to discover in John 14: 5-6. In the second quotation, however, Louis XIV asserts that when his individual self is gone, the State will continue. Jesus' words to Thomas reflect a similar sentiment.

28. "Elaine Pagels' Search for Christ the Mystic," in *Shambhala Sun*, November 2004, p. 103.

29. "Considerations on Keeping Negroes, Part Second," in John Woolman, *The Journal and Major Essays*, ed. Phillips P. Moulton (Richmond, IN Friends United Press, 1980), p. 236.

30. *Lao Tzu: Text, Notes, and Comments*, by Chen Ku-Ying, Translated and Adapted by Rhett Y.W. Young and Roger T. Ames (San Francisco: Chinese Materials Center, Inc. 1977), p. 51.

31. For a scathing account of the historical origins of Christian

anti-Semitism, see James Carroll, *Constantine's Sword: The Church and the Jews—A History* (Mariner, 2001).

32. Brother Lawrence, *The Practice of the Presence of God* (Tappan, NJ: Spire books, 1958, 1979), p. 31.

33. *The Silent Cry: Mysticism and Resistance* (Minneapolis: Fortress Press, 2001), p. 10.

34. Keating, *Seekers of Ultimate Mystery.*

35. *Field Notes on the Compassionate Life*, p. 13.

36. Jack Kornfield, *After the Ecstasy, the Laundry: How the Heart Grows Wise on the Spiritual Path* (New York: Bantam, 2000), p. 124.

37. As a boy, I drew strength to make these choices from a simple little poem, "Outwitted," by Edwin Markham (1852-1940):
    He drew a circle that shut me out
    Heretic, rebel, a thing to flout
    But love and I had wit to win:
    We drew a circle that took him in.

38. See Chapter Two.

39. *The Journal of George Fox*, ed. by John. L. Nickalls (Cambridge: Cambridge University press, 1952), pp. 347f. Quoted and discussed also in Chapter Two, "Be Still and Cool": see above.

40. "Conservative" here designates those independent Yearly Meetings—Iowa, North Carolina, Ohio—that still reflect more strongly than others the cultural and theological flavor of "Quietist" Friends from the 18th through the mid-19th centuries. The word "conservative" does not entail what we now regard as social or political conservatism.

41. Lloyd Lee Wilson, *Holy Surrender*, New England Yearly Meeting Keynote Address, presented eighth month, 2006, with an introduction by Brian Drayton (Wooster, MA: New England Yearly Meeting, 2006).

42. Ibid pp. 4f, 8, 14f, 16.

43. Anselm Gruen, *Heaven Begins Within You: Wisdom from the Desert Fathers*, translated by Peter Heinegg (New York: Crossroads, 1994, 1999), p. 20.

Part II: ILLUMINATION

CHAPTER FOUR:

LIVING PEACE

1. In dating this incident, I follow Peter Brock, *The Quaker Peace Testimony: 1660 to 1914* (York, England: Sessions Book Trust, 1990) p. 14. For an alternative dating, see H. Larry Ingle, *First Among Friends: George Fox and the Creation of Quakerism* (New York and Oxford: Oxford University Press, 1994) p. 67.

2. *The Journal of George Fox*, edited by John L. Nickalls (London: The Religious Society of Friends, 1975) p. 21.

3. Ibid., p. 65.

4. I quote from the *King James Version* here to convey wording that might have been familiar to Fox. *The New Revised Standard Version* reads as follows: "Let everyone be quick to listen, slow to speak, slow to anger; for your anger does not produce God's righteousness... the wisdom from above is first pure, then peaceable, gentle, willing to yield, full of mercy and good fruits, without a trace of partiality or hypocrisy. And a harvest of righteousness is sown in peace for those who make peace. Those conflicts and disputes among you, where do they come from? Do they not come from your cravings that are at war within you? You want something and do not have it; so you commit murder. And you covet something and cannot obtain it; so you engage in disputes and conflicts. You do not have, because you do not ask. You ask and do not receive, because you ask wrongly, in order to spend what you get on your pleasures."

5. "To All That Would Know The Way to The Kingdom" (1653), in *Gospel Truth Demonstrated, in a Collection of Doctrinal Books* (Philadelphia and New York: AMS Press, 1831, 1975), p. 17.

6. See T. Canby Jones, *George Fox's Attitude Toward War* (Annapolis, MD: Academic Fellowship, 1972), pp. 58-60.

7. Fox, *Journal*, p. 11.

8. Fox, p. 12.

9. Fox, p. 17.

10. Fox, p. 21.

11. Fox, p. 27.

12. Fox, p. 126.

13. Fox, pp. 127f.

14. Ingle, p. 94.

15. Fox, *Journal*, p. 129.

16. Fox, pp. 131f.

17. Ibid., p. 240. For a thorough review and analysis of Fox's behavior and testimony regarding violence and war, see T. Canby Jones, *George Fox's Attitude Toward War*.

18. Ingle, p. 93.

19. *Undaunted Zeal: The Letters of Margaret Fell*, edited by Elsa F. Glines (Richmond, IN: Friends United Press, 2003).

20. Ingle, p. 94.

21. Glines, p. 49. I have modernized the period spelling in Glines' edition.

22. Glines, p. 48.

23. Quoted in Ingle, p. 195. According to Ingle, "almost nothing is known about Wilkenson."

24. Mary Garman, Judith Applegate, Margaret Benefiel, and Dortha Meredith, eds. *Hidden in Plain Sight: Quaker Women's Writings 1650-1700* (Wallingford, PA: Pendle Hill Publications, 1996) p. 72. See also pp. 91-93, 105, 108f, 117f. Special thanks to Mary Garman for drawing my attention to these passages.

25. From "A Declaration and an Information from Us, the People of God Called Quakers," in *Margaret Fox, A Brief Collection of Remarkable Passages Relating to... Margaret Fell, 1710*, pp. 208-210. Cited in Quaker Faith and Practice of Britain Yearly Meeting, 19.46.

26. www.quakerhouse.org/pt-reconsider-04.htm.

27. Fox, *Journal*, p. 67.

28. Fox, pp. 197f.

29. Ingle, p. 121f.

30. Ingle, p. 194.

31. Fox, *Journal*, p. 197.

32. Fox, p. 263.

33. Fox, p. 169.

34. Here I follow the retrospective dating of the New Style or Gregorian calendar, adopted in 1752. Following the Old Style or Julian calendar, this event is dated in 1660.

35. www.quakerhouse.org/pt-reconsider-01.htm. I am deeply indebted here to Fager's reconstruction and analysis.

36. www.quakerhouse.org/pt-reconsider-04.htm.

37. Fox, *Journal*, p. 27. This passage reports the key spiritual insight that became known as Friends' doctrine of perfection. See Barclay's Apology In Modern English, edited by Dean Freiday, pp. 155-165.

38. Fox, *Journal*, p. 19.

39. See *Quaker Faith and Practice* of Britain Yearly Meeting, 1948.

40. It is tempting to see these disparate schools of thought as motivated partly by the desire to reclaim just what the Enlightenment sought to deny: the thick-textured particularity of every utterance, reflecting not "universal, abstract truth," but the history and specific experience of the speaker.

41. Wilmer Cooper, *The Testimony of Integrity*, Pendle Hill Pamphlet #296 (Wallingford, PA: Pendle Hill Publications, 1991), p. 38.

42. Principle integrity is compatible with morally abhorrent behavior; whether "living up to one's principles" is admirable depends upon what those principles are. In a speech during World War II, Heinrich Himmler, leader of the S.S., urged a group of Nazi generals as a point of morality to stand by the principle of "extermination of the Jewish race." He justified his principled stand by declaring that "The curse of greatness is that it must step over dead bodies to create new life. Yet we must cleanse the soil or it will never bear fruit." See William Shirer, *The Rise and Fall of the Third Reich* (New York, 1960), pp. 937-938, 966, as well as Roger Manwell and Heinrich Fraenkel, *Heinrich Himmler* (London, 1965), pp. 132, 184, 187, 197.

43. "To All That Would Know the Way to the Kingdom," p. 25.

44. Thanks to David Levering for the insights that inspired this paragraph.

45. *Essays on the Quaker Vision of Gospel Order* (Philadelphia, PA: Quaker Press, 1993), p. 23.

46. In his account of the 1656 incident of physical abuse cited above, Fox reports that he appealed to local authorities for "a magistrate... (that) should show forth gravity, and sobriety, and his authority, and keep the people civil." (See *Journal*, p. 238.) Many years later, when drawing up a constitution for the new territory of Pennsylvania, William Penn provided not only for magistrates authorized to use coercive force to maintain the peace, and for correctional institutions where criminals might be incarcerated, but also for a limited number of crimes punishable by execution.

47. For a telling indictment of the present system of criminal justice (including a proposal to abandon entirely the use of prisons), see Laura Magnani and Harmon L. Wray, *Beyond Prisons: A New Interfaith Paradigm for Our Failed Prison System* (Minneapolis: Fortress Press, 2006).

48. Special thanks to the ministry of Friend Mary Cooper for the original of this image.

CHAPTER FIVE:

HEALING GENDER HURT

1. "The Man with a Hoe." Readily available online. Markam wrote the poem in 1899 in response to the famous painting by Jean-Francois Millet.

2. See Chapter Four, "Living Peace," for a fuller account of my boyhood struggles with violence.

3. Among the titles used in the final version of the course (1995) were Deborah Tannen, *You Just Don't Understand: Women and Men in Conversation* (Ballantine 1990); Alison M. Jaggar & Paul S. Rothenberg, *Feminist Frameworks: Alternative Theoretical Accounts of the Relations Between Women and Men, Third Edition* (McGraw-Hill 1993); Terry Kupers, *Revisioning Men's Lives: Gender, Intimacy, and Power* (Guilford 1993); and Aaron Kipnis & Elizabeth Herron, *What Women and Men Really Want* (Nataraj 1995).

4. The primary texts for this course were Michael Kimmel and Michael Messner's *Men's Lives* (Macmillan 1989, 1995) and David Gilmore, *Manhood in the Making: Cultural Concepts of Masculinity* (New Haven, CT: Yale University Press, 1990).

5. Quoted in *Encyclopedia of Philosophy*, Vol. 6: "Power" by Stanley I. Benn (New York: Macmillan, 1967), p. 424.

6. Kenneth E. Boulding, *Three Faces of Power* (London: Sage, 1990).

7. David Gilmore, *Manhood in the Making: Cultural Concepts of Masculinity* (New Haven, Conn.: Yale University Press, 1990).

8. Ibid., p. 219.

9. Ibid., p. 203.

10. Ibid., p. 206.

11. Ibid., p. 224.

12. Ibid., p. 210.

13. Ibid., p. 211.

14. Ibid., p. 223.

15. Ibid., p. 223.

16. Herb Goldberg, *The New Male: From Destruction to Self-Care* (New York: Signet, 1979), p. 12.

17. These themes are richly explored in Catherine Keller's *From a Broken Web: Separation, Sexism and Self* (Boston: Beacon Press, 1986).

18. *BJS Data Report, 1989*, U. S. Department of Justice Bureau of Justice Statistics, NCJ-121514, p. 80.

19. Shepherd Bliss, "The Mythopoetic Approach to Men," AXIS, no. 4 (Winter, 1989-90), p. 1.

20. For an extensive, well-documented discussion of such strategies, see Myriam Miedzian, *Boys Will Be Boys: Breaking the Link Between Masculinity and Violence* (New York: Anchor Books, 1991).

21. John Calvi, "Facing sexual hurt," letter to *Friends Journal*, April 1998, p. 5.

22. See Herb Goldberg, *The Hazards of Being Male: Surviving the Myths of Masculine Privilege* (New York: signet, 1976), esp. Chapter 12; James Harrison, James Chin, and Thomas Ficarrotto, "Warning: Masculinity May be Dangerous to Your Health," in *Men's Lives*, ed. by Michael S. Kimmel and Michael Messner, pp. 296-309 (New York: Macmillan, 1989); *American Health* (January/February 1989), pp. 62f.

CHAPTER SIX:

FRIENDLY PEDAGOGY

1. "Meeting for Worship for Business," in *Faith and Practice: A Guide to Quaker Discipline in the Experience of Pacific Yearly Meeting of the Religious Society of Friends* (Pacific Yearly Meeting, 2001), p. 31.

2. This self-discovery was greatly aided by my involvement with the Friends Association for Higher Education (FAHE), an affiliation of Quaker-related colleges and universities, as well as Quaker (and Quaker-friendly) staff and faculty from non-Quaker schools, which holds annual conferences on the campuses of its member institutions. For some ten years I was actively involved in FAHE, simultaneously challenged and supported by this marvelous community. See http://quakerfahe.com/.

3. See the classic two-volume study of Quaker spirituality by Patricia Loring, *Listening Spirituality, Vol. I: Personal Spiritual Practices Among Friends and Vol. II: Corporate Spiritual Practices Among Friends* (Philadelphia, PA: QuakerBooks of Friends General Conference, 1997 and 1999).

4. See especially Paul. A. Lacey, *Growing Into Goodness: Essays on Quaker Education* (Wallingford, PA: Pendle Hill Publications, 1998) and *Education and the Inward Teacher*, Pendle Hill Pamphlet #278 (Wallingford, PA: Pendle Hill Publications, 1988); Parker Palmer, *Meeting for Learning: Education in a Quaker Context*, Pendle Hill Bulletin No. 284 (Wallingford, PA: Pendle Hill, 1976), *To Know As We Are Known: A Spirituality of Education* (New York: Harper & Row, 1983), *The Courage To Teach: Exploring The Inner Landscape of a Teacher's Life* (San Francisco: Jossey-Bass, 1998); Douglas H. Heath, *Schools of Hope: Developing Mind and Character in Today's Youth* (San Francisco: Jossey-Bass, 1994); Helen Hole, *Things Civil and Useful* (Richmond, IN: Friends United Press, 1978); Kim Hays, *Practicing Virtues: Moral Traditions at Quaker and Military Boarding Schools* (Berkeley: University of California Press, 1994).

5. I take this "banking" metaphor from Paulo Freire, *Pedagogy of the Oppressed* (New York: Continuum, 1999), p. 72.

6. Plato, *The Republic, Book VII*, 518 c-d.

7. Parker Palmer, "Meeting for Learning," p. 3.

8. "Making Science Stick," in *Harvard Magazine*, July-August 2012, p. 8f.

9. R. Melvin Keiser, *Inward Light and the New Creation: A Theological Meditation on the Center and Circumference of Quakerism*. Pendle Hill Pamphlet #295. (Wallingford, PA.: Pendle Hilll Publications, 1991), p. 8.

10. Jessamyn West, ed., *The Quaker Reader* (New York: Viking Press, 1962), pp. 213f.

11. Nelle Morton, *The Journey Is Home* (Boston: Beacon Press, 1985), p. 128.

12. Margaret Hope Bacon, *Mothers of Feminism: The Story of Quaker Women in America* (San Francisco: Harper & Row, Publishers, 1986), p. 1.

13. Parker Palmer, *The Courage to Teach: Exploring the Inner Landscape of a Teacher's Life* (San Francisco: Jossey-Bass, 1998), p. 117.

14. Robert K. Greenleaf, *Servant Leadership: A Journey Into the Nature of Legitimate Power and Greatness* (New York: Paulist Press, 1977), p.13f.

15. Frederick B. Tolles and E. Gordon Alderfer, eds., *The Witness of William Penn* (New York: Macmillan, 1957), p.189.

16. Peter Brock, *The Quaker Peace Testimony: 1660 to 1914* (York, England: Sessions book Trust, 1990), pp. 27-30, 322 n. 5. See Chapter Four, "Living Peace," for a fuller discussion of the historical origins and meaning of the Quaker Peace Testimony.

Part III: UNION

CHAPTER SEVEN:

IN THE LOVE OF NATURE

1. "Emro Farm," privately published manuscript. Margaret Lacey (my sister) has published a collection of stories spanning three generations of a Quaker family who live on the farm on which she and I were raised: *Silent Friends: A Quaker Quilt* (Urbana, IL: Stormline Press, 1992). Available through Pendle Hill and FGC Bookstores.

2. Henry David Thoreau, *Walden*, many editions.

3. In *The End of Nature* (New York: Random House, 1989), noted

environmental author Bill McKibben explores the many dimensions of this tragedy.

4. Mahlon Hoagland and Bert Dodson, *The Way Life Works* (New York: Times Books, 1995), p. 26. Quoted in Paul Hawken, *Blessed Unrest: How the Largest Movement in the World Came into Being and Why No One Saw It Coming* (New York: Viking, 2007), p. 183.

5. *A Path With Heart: A Guide Through the Perils and Promises of Spiritual Life* (New York: Bantam, 1993), p. 24.

6. From "A Plea for the Poor," John Woolman, *The Journal and Major Essays*, ed. Phillips P. Moulton, 1971 (Richmond, IN: Friends United Press, 1989), p. 241.

7. Paul Hawken, *Blessed Unrest: How the Largest Movement in the World Came into Being and Why No One Saw It Coming*, (New York: Viking, 2007), p. 131.

8. Anthony Manousos and Eric Sabelman, "The Genesis of Earthlight and of the Quaker Environmental Movement," in *Earthlight: Spiritual Wisdom for an Ecological Age*, edited by Cindy Spring and Anthony Manousos with Eric Sabelman and Sandy Farley (Oakland, CA; Friends Bulletin Corporation, 2007), p. 19.

9. "Tender Mercies" in "the earthwitness journal" (http://journal.earthwitness.org/), posted 2 July 2007.

10. In addition to the main text, a powerful, comprehensive statement of the state of the environmental movement, Hawken and his associates have provided a useful typology of the many thousands of nonprofit organizations around the globe whose work bears upon earthcare. The appendix runs to more than 110 pages. See also the web site for WISER—the *World Index of Social and Environmental Responsibility*, at www.wiserearth.org.

11. Ibid., pp. 3, 4.

12. Keith Helmuth, in "Friends Testimonies and Ecological Understanding," thoughtfully explores the extension of Friends' testimonies to many dimensions of the "human-earth relationship." See *Friends Journal*, December 2007, pp. 14-17.

13. Robert E. Hinshaw, "Managing Conflict and Natural Resources through Good Clerking: The Legacy of Gilbert F. White," in *Friends Journal*, April 2007 (Vol. 53, No. 4), p. 13. My observations about the life and work of Gilbert White are drawn from this fine article.

14. Ibid., p. 15.

15. *The Journal of George Fox*, John L. Nickalls, ed. (Cambridge: Cambridge University Press, 1952), p. 27.

16. *The Wisdom of Wilderness: Experiencing the Healing Power of Nature*, with a Foreword by Parker J. Palmer (San Francisco: HarperSanFrancisco, 2006), p. 188.

17. Ibid., p. 75.

18. Ibid., p. 85.

19. "A Christian Vision of the Earth," in *Friends Journal*, April 2007, p. 11.

20. From *A Sand County Almanac*, excerpted in Luis P. Pojman, *Environmental Ethics: Readings in Theory and Application*, 3rd Edition (Belmont, CA: Wadsworth, 2001), p. 120.

21. David C. Korten, *The Great Turning: From Empire to Earth Community* (Bloomfield, CT and San Francisco: Kumarian Press, Inc. and Berrett-Koehler Publishers, Inc., 2006), p. 22.

22. See Christopher Hill, *The World Turned Upside Down: Radical Ideas During the English Revolution* (London: Penguin 1972) for a classic social history of the period.

23. See Dominique Lapierre, *The City of Joy* (New York: Warner Books, 1985).

24. Fox, *Journal*, p. 11.

CHAPTER EIGHT:
JOYFUL WITNESS

1. Fredrick Buechner, *Wishful Thinking: A Theological ABC* (San Francisco, CA: HarperSanFrancisco, 1973, 1993), p. 95.

2. The Dalai Lama, *The Art of Happiness*, quoted by Bodhipaksa: "If you want others to be happy, practice compassion." www.wildmind.org/blog, posted 16 May 2007.

3. Day borrowed this phrase from John Ruskin, *The True and the Beautiful in Nature, Art, Morals and Religion* (New York: Merrill and Baker, 1858) and uses it frequently in her personal diaries. See Dorothy Day, *The Duty of Delight: The Diaries of Dorothy Day*, ed. by Robert Ellsberg (Milwaukee, WI: Marquette University press, 2008).

4. Bodhipaksa, ibid.

5. Ibid.

6. *Finding Flow: The Psychology of Engagement with Everyday Life* (New York: Basic Books, 1997), pp. 131f.

7   *Man and Superman: Epistle Dedicatory* (New York: Brendan's, 1903), p. xxxif.

8. *New York: Broadway Books*, 2007, p. 1.

9. Ibid., p. 2.

10. *The Dhammapada* is one of the best-known texts from the Theravada Buddhist tradition, ascribed to the Buddha himself. This verse comes from Chapter One (many translations).

11. Paul Knitter, *Without Buddha I Could Not be a Christian (Oxford, One World*, 2009), p. 208f.

12. Ibid.

13. "An Enemy Is One Whose Story We Have Not Heard," in *Fellowship: The Journal of the Fellowship of Reconciliation*, May/June 1997. In 1996, some eighteen persons, including Hoffman herself, traveled to Israel and Palestine on behalf of the "Compassionate Listening Project," a process of listening to all sides non-judgmentally and non-adversarily. (This article was found online on 30 April 2012.)

14. Pema Chodron, *Taking the Leap: Freeing Ourselves from Old Habits and Fears* (Boston and London: Shambhala, 2010), p. 86.

15. Fox, *Journal*, p. 28.

16. Donations were collected into what became known as the Kendal Fund.

17. "To Friends in the North 1654," reprinted in *Undaunted Zeal: The Letters of Margaret Fell*, edited and introduced by Elsa F. Glines (Richmond, IN: Friends United Press, 2003), pp. 89-91. Spelling has been modernized.

18. The preceding four paragraphs have been adapted from my essay, "My Yoke Is easy, and My Burden is Light," in *Hearing Each Other Into Speech: Doing Theology at Pilgrim Place, Vol. 6: 2010-2011*, ed. by Paul Kittlaus, Pat Patterson, Donna Blackstone (Shelbyville, KY: Wasteland Press, 2011), pp. 19-21. Used with permission.

19. *The Journal and Major Essays of John Woolman*, ed. by Phillips P.

Moulton (Richmond, IN: Friends United Press, 1980), pp. 92f.

20. Ibid., pp. 112, 157.

21. Quoted in Margaret Hope Bacon, *Mothers of Feminism: The Story of Quaker Women in America* (San Francisco: Harper and Row, 1986), p.116.

22. See Elizabeth Gray Vining, *Friend of Life: A Biography of Rufus M. Jones* (Philadelphia: Philadelphia Yearly Meeting, 1958), p. 172. As an exchange student at the Freie Universitat in Berlin in 1959-60, I received from Germans grateful acknowledgement of "Quakerspeise" following the war.

23. Vining, p. 282.

24. Ibid., pp. 290f.

25. Ibid., pp. 286, 289, 291.

26. Ibid., p. 293.

27. *A Testament of Devotion* (New York: HarperOne, 1941, 1992), p. 83.

28. See Gregg Levoy, *Callings: Finding and Following an Authentic Life* (New York: Random House, 1997), p. 6.

29. See "Five Tests for Discerning a True Leading," Hugh Barbour, *The Quakers in Puritan England* (New Haven, CT: Yale University Press, 1964), pp. 119-123.

30. The preceding four paragraphs are adapted from *Faithfulness In Action: Supporting Leadings in Pacific Yearly Meeting, Draft 2.2* (June 2009). Unpublished; no copyright. Drafted by myself with excellent editorial support from Elaine Emily, Melissa Lovett-Adair, Carl Magruder and Sue Torrey.

31. These three paragraphs are adapted from my "'Leadings' for Nontheistic Friends?" in *Friends Journal*, Vol. 57, No. 1 (January 2011) (Philadelphia, PA: Friends Publishing Corp.)

32. Nancy Bieber, *Decision Making & Spiritual Discernment: The Sacred Art of Finding Your Way* (Woodstock, VT: 2010, SkyLight Paths Publishing), p. 6. See also J. Brent Bill, *Sacred Compass: The Way of Spiritual Discernment* (Brewster, MA: Paraclete Press, 2008); Gregg Levoy, *Callings: Finding and following an Authentic Life* (New York: Three Rivers Press, 1997); Parker Palmer, *Let Your Life Speak: Listening for the Voice of Vocation* (San Francisco: Jossey-Bass, Inc., 2000) and *A Hidden Wholeness: The Journey*

Toward An Undivided Life; Welcoming the Soul and Weaving Community in a Wounded World (San Francisco: Jossey Bass, 2004). In the latter book, Palmer develops an elaborated version of the traditional Quaker practice of "clearness committees." (Bieber, Bill, and Palmer are Friends.)

33. This theme was explored in Chapter Three, "Pure Passion."

34. Murray, *The Scottish Himalayan Expedition, 1951.*

35. This is the title of a book on Taoism by Alan Watts.

36. Bieber, p. 164.

37. *Holy Surrender*, New England Yearly Meeting Keynote Address, presented eighth month, 2006, with an introduction by Brian Drayton (Wooster, MA: New England Yearly Meeting, 2006), p. 16.

CHAPTER NINE:
WALKING CHEERFULLY

1. Pema Chodron, *Living Beautifully with Uncertainty and Change* (Boston and London: Shambhala, 2012), p. 37

2. Wallace Stevens, *The Poems of Our Climate*. The entire stanza reads as follows:
   There would still remain the never-resting mind,
   So that one would want to escape, come back
   To what had been so long composed.
   The imperfect is our paradise.
   Note that, in this bitterness, delight,
   Since the imperfect is so hot in us,
   Lies in flawed words and stubborn sounds.

3. Albert Camus, *The Myth of Sisyphus and Other Essays*, translated by Justin O'Brien (New York: Vintage, 1959), p. 90.

4. *Rumi*, quoted in Dorothee Soelle, *The Silent Cry: Mysticism and Resistance* (Minneapolis, MN: Fortress Press, 2001), p. 34.

5. This and subsequent quotations from Eva Hermann, "In Prison—Yet Free." Found online at http://www.tractassociation.org/InPrisonYetFree.html.

6. Viktor Frankl, *Man's Search for Meaning: An Introduction to Logotherapy* (New York: Pocket Books, 1959, 1971), p. 54.

7. Ibid., pp. 58f. Emphasis in original.

8. Ibid., pp. 124, 114.

9. Albert Camus, *The Myth of Sisyphus and Other Essays* (New York: Vintage: 1959), p. 38.

10. Ibid., p. 91.

11. Pun intended.

12. From Dedication to Chapter 10 of the *Bodhicharyavatara of Master Shantideva*. Found in "Shantideva's Dedication Prayer." Official Website of His Eminence Tsem Tulku Rinpoche, posted June 5, 2009. Shantideva was an 8th-century Indian Buddhist Scholar who adhered to the philosophy of Nagarjuna.

13. Jack Kornfield, *A Path with Heart* (Bantam 1993), pp. 11, 14, 19. Emphasis in original.

14. George Fox, Epistle #131 (1656) in T*he Power of the Lord Is Over All: The Pastoral Letters of George Fox*, ed. by T. Canby Jones (Richmond, IN: Friends United Press, 1989), p. 101f.

15. Isaac Penington, 1667; quoted in *Quaker Faith and Practice* (London: The Yearly Meeting of the Religious Society of Friends (Quakers) in Britain, 1999), 10.01.

16. The concept of original sin—a notion that has always seemed to me inherently abusive—may be an attempt to render this experiential reality in theological terms.

17. Fra Giovanni Giocondo (c. 1435-1515) was a Franciscan friar, an architect, engineer, and classical scholar. This passage is a portion of his letter to Countess Allagia Aldobrandeschi on Christmas Eve, 1513. From Gratefulness.org; 31 October 2012.

18. In *The Uttermost Deep: The Challenge of Near-Death Experiences* (New York: Lantern Books, 2001), Friend Gracia Fay Ellwood carefully analyzes many reports of near-death experiences to determine what support they provide for the hypothesis of an afterlife. Ellwood's nuanced conclusion is that the evidence favors such an hypothesis.

19. I borrow this observation from Anselm Gruen, *Heaven Begins Within You: Wisdom from the Desert Fathers* (New York: Crossroads, 1994, 2011), p. 21.

20. Rita Nakashima Brock and Rebecca Ann Parker, *Saving Paradise: How Christianity Traded Love of This World for Crucifrixion and Empire* (Boston: Beacon Press, 2008), pp. xv, 25.

21. I am well aware of the androcentric and hierarchical connotations of this phrase. I retain it for reasons of historical clarity, while reconstruing it inclusively as the "Kin-dom of God."

22. Gerard Guiton, "Recovering the Lost Radiance: The Kingdom of God, the Early Friends, and the Future of Quakerism," in *Quaker Religious Thought, Cumulative No. 113* (December 2009) (Newberg, OR: 2009), p. 33.

23. Gerard Guiton, *The Early Friends and the "Kingdom of God": Peace, Testimony and Revolution* (San Francisco: Inner Light Books, 2012), p. 150.

24. Ibid., p. 161.

25. *A Path With Heart: A Guide Through the Perils and Promises of Spiritual Life* (New York: Bantam, 1993), pp. 332-334, 336.

26. *Living Zen, Loving God* (Boston: Wisdom Publications, 2004), pp. X, 6. For a careful exploration of these themes from an evangelical Friend's point of view, see Arthur O. Roberts, *Messengers of God: The Sensuous Side of Spirituality* (Newberg, OR: Barclay Press, 1996).

27. Quoted in *Quaker Faith & Practice, Second Edition* (London: The Yearly Meeting of the Religious Society of Friends in Britain, 1995, 1999), 26.04.

28. Rumi, "Melting Snow," in *The Essential Rumi*, translations by Coleman Barks (San Francisco: HarperSanFrancisco, 1995), p. 13

29. Sakyong Mipham Rinpoche, "A Simple Sense of Delight," in *Shambhala Sun*, November 2003, p. 12.

30. Ibid.

31. Sylvia Boorstein, "Living in the Divine Abodes," in *Shambhala Sun*, January 2008, p. 71.

32. *Journal*, p. 263.

BIBLIOGRAPHY

Ambler, Rex, *Truth of the Heart: An Anthology of George Fox* (London: Quaker Books, 2001)

Armstrong, Karen, *The Case for God* (New York: Knopf, 2009)

Bacon, Margaret Hope, Mothers of Feminism: The Story of Quaker Women in America (San Francisco: Harper & Row, Publishers, 1986)

Barasch, Marc Ian, *Field Notes on the Compassionate Life: A Search for the Soul of Kindness* (Rodale, 2005)

Barbour, Hugh, *The Quakers in Puritan England* (New Haven: Yale University Press, 1964)

Beck, Charlotte Joko, *Everyday Zen: Love and Work*, ed. by Steve Smith (San Francisco: HarperOne, 1989)

_____, *Nothing Special: Living Zen*, ed. by Steve Smith (San Francisco: HarperOne 1993)

Bieber, Nancy, *Decision Making & Spiritual Discernment: The Sacred Art of Finding Your Way* (Woodstock, VT: 2010, SkyLight Paths Publishing)

Bill, J. Brent, *Sacred Compass: The Way of Spiritual Discernment* (Brewster, MA: Paraclete Press, 2008)

Brock, Peter, *The Quaker Peace Testimony: 1660 to 1914* (York, England: Sessions Book Trust, 1990)

Brother Lawrence, *The Practice of the Presence of God* (Tappan, NJ: Spire books, 1958, 1979)

Boulding, Kenneth E., *Three Faces of Power* (London: Sage, 1990)

Bownas, Samuel, *A Description of the Qualifications Necessary to a Gospel Minister* (Philadelphia: Pendle Hill Publications and Tract Association of Friends, 1989)

Brinton, Howard, *Friends for 300 Years: The History and Beliefs of the Society of Friends since George Fox started the Quaker movement* (Wallingford, PA: Pendle Hill Publications, 1952)

Brock, Rita Nakashima, and Rebecca Ann Parker, *Saving Paradise: How Christianity Traded Love of This World for Crucifixion and Empire* (Boston: Beacon Press, 2008)

Camus, Albert, *The Myth of Sisyphus and Other Essays*, trans. by Justin O'Brien (New York: Vintage, 1959)

Chodron, Pema, *Taking the Leap: Freeing Ourselves from Old Habits and Fears*, ed. by Sandy Boucher (Boston & London: Shambhala, 2010)

Cooper, Wilmer, *The Testimony of Integrity*, Pendle Hill Pamphlet #296 (Wallingford, PA: Pendle Hill Publications, 1991)

Csikszentmihalyi, Mihaly, *Finding Flow: The Psychology of Engagement with Everyday Life* (New York: Basic Books, 1997)

Day, Dorothy, *The Duty of Delight: The Diaries of Dorothy Day*, ed. by Robert Ellsberg (Milwaukee, WI: Marquette University press, 2008)

Dumoulin, Heinrich, S.J., *A History of Zen Buddhism* (Boston: Beacon Press, 1963)

Ellwood, Gracia Fay, *The Uttermost Deep: The Challenge of Near-Death Experiences* (New York: Lantern Books, 2001)

Faith and Practice: A Guide to Quaker Discipline in the Experience of Pacific Yearly Meeting of the Religious Society of Friends (Pacific Yearly Meeting, 2001)

Fell, Margaret, *Undaunted Zeal: The Letters of Margaret Fell*, Elsa Glines, ed. (Richmond, IN: Friends United Press, 2003)

Fox, George, *Journal of George Fox*, ed. by John L. Nickalls (London: Religious Society of Friends, 1975)

_____, *"The Power of the Lord Is Over All": The Pastoral Letters of George Fox*, Introduced and edited by T. Canby Jones (Richmond, IN: Friends United Press, 1989)

Frankl, Viktor, *Man's Search for Meaning: An Introduction to Logotherapy* (New York: Pocket Books, 1959, 1971)

Garman, Mary, Judith Applegate, Margaret Benefiel, Dorothy Meredith, eds., *Hidden in Plain Sight: Quaker Women's Writings 1656–1700* (Wallingford, PA: Pendle Hill Publications, 1996)

Gilmore, David, *Manhood in the Making: Cultural Concepts of Masculinity* (New Haven, Conn.: Yale University Press, 1990)

Greenleaf, Robert K., *Servant Leadership: A Journey Into the Nature of Legitimate Power and Greatness* (New York: Paulist Press, 1977)

Gruen, Anselm, *Heaven Begins Within You: Wisdom from the Desert Fathers*, trans. by Peter Heinegg (New York: Crossroads, 1994, 1999)

Guiton, Gerard, "Recovering the Lost Radiance: The Kingdom of God, the Early Friends, and the Future of Quakerism," in *Quaker Religious Thought*, Cum. No. 113 (Newberg, OR: 2009)

_____, *The Early Friends and the "Kingdom of God": Peace, Testimony and Revolution* (San Francisco: Inner Light Books, 2012)

Gwyn, Douglas, *Unmasking the Idols: A Journey Among Friends* (Richmond, IN: Friends United Press, 1989)

_____, *The Covenant Crucified: Quakers and the Rise of Capitalism* (Wallingford, PA: Pendle Hill Publications, 1995)

_____, *Seekers Found: Atonement in Early Quaker Experience* (Wallingford, PA: Pendle Hill Publications, 2000)

Habito, Ruben, *Living Zen, Loving God* (Boston: Wisdom Publications, 2004)

Hawken, Paul, *Blessed Unrest: How the Largest Movement in the World Came into Being and Why No One Saw It Coming* (New York: Viking, 2007)

Ingle, H. Larry, *First Among Friends: George Fox and the Creation of Quakerism* (New York and Oxford: Oxford University Press, 1994)

James, William, *The Varieties of Religious Experience: A Study in Human Nature* (New York: Mentor, 1958)

Jones, T. Canby, *George Fox's Attitude Toward War* (Annapolis, MD: Academic Fellowship, 1972)

Kabat-Zinn, Jon, *Coming to Our Senses: Healing Ourselves and the World Through Mindfulness* (New York: Hyperion, 2005)

Kasimow, Harold, John P. Keenan, and Linda Klepinger Keenan, eds., *Beside Still Waters: Jews, Christians, and the Way of the Buddha* (Boston: Wisdom Publications, 2003)

Keiser, R. Melvin, *Inward Light and the New Creation: A Theological Meditation on the Center and Circumference of Quakerism*, Pendle Hill Pamphlet #295. (Wallingford, PA.: Pendle Hill Publications, 1991)

Keller, Catherine, *From a Broken Web: Separation, Sexism and Self* (Boston: Beacon Press, 1986)

Kelly, Thomas, *A Testament of Devotion* (New York: HarperOne, 1941, 1992)

Kennedy, Robert, Zen Spirit, *Christian Spirit: The Place of Zen in Christian Life* (New York: Continuum, 1995, 2001)

Knitter, Paul F., *Without Buddha I Could not be a Christian* (Oxford: Oneworld Publications, 2009)

Kornfield, Jack, *A Path with Heart: A Guide Through the Perils and Promises of Spiritual Life* (New York: Bantam,1993)

_____, *After the Ecstasy, the Laundry: How the Heart Grows Wise on the Spiritual Path* (New York: Bantam, 2000)

Korten, David C., *The Great Turning: From Empire to Earth Community* (Bloomfield, CT and San Francisco: Kumarian Press, Inc. and Berrett-Koehler Publishers, Inc., 2006)

Lacey, Paul. A., *Education and the Inward Teacher*, Pendle Hill Pamphlet #278 (Wallingford, PA: Pendle Hill Publications, 1988)

_____, *Growing Into Goodness: Essays on Quaker Education* (Wallingford, PA: Pendle Hill Publications, 1998)

Lao Tzu: Text, Notes, and Comments, by Chen Ku-Ying, translated and adapted by Rhett Y. W. Young and Roger T. Ames (San Francisco: Chinese Materials Center, Inc., 1977)

Levoy, Gregg, *Callings: Finding and Following an Authentic Life* (New York: Random House, 1997)

Loring, Patricia, *Listening Spirituality, Volume I: Personal Spiritual Practices Among Friends* (Washington DC: Opening Press, 1977)

_____, *Listening Spirituality, Volume II: Corporate Spiritual Practice Among Friends* (Washington DC: Opening Press, 1999).

Magid, Barry, *Ending the Pursuit of Happiness: A Zen Guide* (Boston: Wisdom Publications, 2008)

May, Gerald, *The Wisdom of Wilderness: Experiencing the Healing Power of Nature*, with a Foreword by Parker J. Palmer (San Francisco: HarperSanFrancisco, 2006)

Palmer, Parker, *Meeting for Learning: Education in a Quaker Context*, Pendle Hill Bulletin No. 284 (Wallingford, PA: Pendle Hill, 1976)

_____, *To Know As We Are Known: A Spirituality of Education* (New York: Harper & Row, 1983)

_____, *The Courage To Teach: Exploring The Inner Landscape of a Teacher's Life* (San Francisco: Jossey-Bass, 1998)

_____, *A Hidden Wholeness: The Journey Toward An Undivided Life; Welcoming the Soul and Weaving Community in a Wounded World* (San Francisco: Jossey Bass, 2004)

Penington, Isaac, *Knowing the Mystery of Life Within: Selected Writings of Isaac Penington in their Historical and Theological Context*, selected and introduced by R. Melvin Keiser and Rosemary Moore (London: Quaker Books, 2005)

Punshon, John, *Encounter With Silence: Reflections from the Quaker Tradition* (Richmond IN: Friends United Press, 1987)

Smith, Steve, ed., *Ways of Wisdom: Readings on the Good Life* (Lanham MD: University Press of America 1983)

_____, *A Quaker in the Zendo*, Pendle Hill Pamphlet #370 (Wallingford PA: Pendle Hill Publications, 2003)

_____, *Living in Virtue, Declaring Against War*, Pendle Hill Pamphlet #378 (Wallingford PA: Pendle Hill Publications, 2005)

_____, *In the Love of Nature*, Annual Michener Lecture 2008 (Melbourne Beach FL: Southeastern Yearly Meeting of Religious Society of Friends, 2008)

Soelle, Dorothy, *The Silent Cry: Mysticism and Resistance* (Minneapolis: Fortress Press, 2001)

Spring, Cindy and Anthony Manousos with Eric Sabelman and Sandy Farley, eds., *Earthlight: Spiritual Wisdom for an Ecological Age* (Oakland, CA; Friends Bulletin Corporation, 2007)

Wilson, Lloyd Lee, *Essays on the Quaker Vision of Gospel Order* (Philadelphia, PA: Quaker Press, 1993)

_____, *Holy Surrender*, New England Yearly Meeting Keynote Address, presented eighth month, 2006, with an introduction by Brian Drayton (Wooster, MA: New England Yearly Meeting, 2006)

Woolman, John, *The Journal and Major essays*, ed. Phillips P. Moulton (Richmond, IN: Friends United Press, 1980)

PERMISSIONS

Although written with the intent of eventual inclusion in this book, portions of the manuscript appeared earlier in other publications:

Chapters One and **Two** are adapted from A Quaker in the Zendo, Pendle Hill Pamphlet #370 (Wallingford, PA: Pendle Hill Publications). Copyright © 2003 by Pendle Hill. Used with permission.

An earlier version of **Chapter Three** appeared in: *Doing Theology at Pilgrim Place*, Vol. 8, ed. by Paul Kittlaus, Pat Patterson, Connie Kimos (Shelbyville, KY: Wasteland Press) Copyright © Paul Kittlaus and Pat Patterson, 2013). Used with permission.

Chapter Four is adapted from *Living in Virtue, Declaring Against War: The Spiritual Roots of the Peace Testimony*, Pendle Hill Pamphlet #378 (Wallingford, PA: Pendle Hill Publications). Copyright © 2005 by Pendle Hill. Used with permission.

Chapter Five is adapted from two publications:

1) "Healing Gender Hurt" from February 1993 issue of *Friends Journal*. Copyright © 1993 Friends Publishing Corporation. Used with permission. To subscribe: www.friendsjournal.org

2) "Fear and Power in the Lives of Men" from *Redeeming Men: Religion and Masculinity*, ed. by Stephen B. Boyd, W. Merle Longwood, and Mark W. Muesse. Copyright © Westminster John Knox Press 1996. Used with permission.

Chapter Six is adapted from "The Spiritual Roots of Quaker Pedagogy" in *Minding the Light: Essays in Friendly Pedagogy*, ed. by Anne Dalke and Barbara Dixson (New York: Peter Lang). Copyright © 2004 Peter Lang Publishing, Inc. Used with permission.

Chapter Seven is adapted from *In the Love of Nature*, The Thirty-eighth Michener Quaker Lecture in Florida (Melbourne Beach, FL). Copyright © 2008 by Southeastern Yearly Meeting of the Religious Society of Friends. Used with permission.

Brief portions of **Chapter Eight** and **Chapter Nine** are drawn from "My Yoke Is Easy, and My Burden is Light," in *Hearing Each Other Into Speech: Doing Theology at Pilgrim Place*, Vol. 6: 2010-2011, ed. by Paul Kitlaus, Pat Patterson, Donna Blackstock (Shelbyville, KY; Wasteland Press). Copyright © Paul Kittlaus and Pat Patterson. Used with permission.

ABOUT THE AUTHOR

STEVE SMITH was born in 1939 into an Iowa Quaker farm family, graduated from Scattergood Friends School and Earlham College, and earned a doctorate in Philosophy from Harvard University in 1972. For forty years he taught in the Department of Philosophy and Religious Studies at Claremont McKenna College, specializing in applied ethics. Among his publications are three edited books: a textbook, *WAYS OF WISDOM: Readings on the Good Life* (University Press of America, 1983), and two collections of talks on Zen practice by the American Zen teacher, Charlotte Joko Beck—*EVERYDAY ZEN: Love and Work* (HarperSanFrancisco, 1989), and *NOTHING SPECIAL: Living Zen* (1993). Steve has led Quaker adult education courses and retreats in numerous settings, including Quaker Center (Ben Lomond, CA) and Pendle Hill (Philadelphia, PA).

Steve has served as the presiding clerk for Claremont Monthly Meeting of Friends, Southern California Quarterly Meeting, the Executive Committee of the Friends Association for Higher Education, the Pendle Hill General Board, and Pacific Yearly Meeting. Steve has a son, David, and a step-daughter, Kathy. Now retired, Steve and his second wife Pat, live at Pilgrim Place, a retirement community in Claremont, California. He and Pat have six grandchildren. He can be reached at ssmith@cmc.edu.

INDEX

QUPUBISHING
Quaker Universalist Fellowship
UniversalistFriends.org

REVIEWS

S teve Smith tells of a march on the 25th anniversary of the
bombing of Hiroshima and Nagasaki, painting a vivid image of
the "solemn, self-important Quakers" and the "laughing Buddhists"
marching side by side. His question, "which of us better served
world peace?" is a sharp reminder to pay attention to the depths of
the Quaker tradition. Early Friends knew joy, singing even while
imprisoned in horrid conditions. Through this and other stories,
Smith reveals how training in Zen Buddhism reopened him not only
to a fuller awareness of his Quaker heritage but also to the living,
cheerful reality of Quakerism today. Freely mixing words of Buddhist
writers with biblical passages, he infuses fresh meaning into familiar
Quaker teachings. Through his life story, Smith reveals the power
of spiritual practices that awaken us to our immersion in God's
love—the healing that melds inward and outward dimensions of life,
opening our hearts to justice and mercy.

> —Margery Post Abbott, a released Friend from
> Multnomah Friend's Meeting in Portland,
> Oregon, author of *A Certain Kind of Perfection,*
> *Christianity and the Inner Life,* and *To Be Broken*
> *and Tender: A Quaker Theology for Today.*

S teve Smith writes with clarity and humility, wisdom and
empathy. His testimony to the harmony of Buddhist,
Christian and Quaker paths is highly integrative, borne of his
own deep soul-searching and his commitment to personal
spiritual practice over many years. With poignancy and
breadth of vision, he blends personal journey with larger
insights and scholarship. . . . an important contribution to
Friends and others in this new century.

> —Douglas Gwyn, Quaker pastor and
> scholar of early Quakerism, author of
> *The Covenant Crucified: Quakers* and the
> *Rise of Capitalism and Seekers Found:*
> *Atonement in Early Quaker Experience.*

REVIEWS, cont.

Steve Smith writes beautifully, and the interweaving of personal experience with an inclusive account of religious experience is superb.

> —John Cobb, Professor Emeritus of Theology and
> Prcess Studies, Claremont School of Theology

Profoundly Christian, profoundly Quaker, with much Buddhist inspiration and assistance, Smith digs deeply into the meaning of a life lived in the Quaker spirit that takes away "the occasion of all wars."

> —Sallie B. King, Professor of Religion,
> James Madison University

Read as spiritual autobiography, Steven Smith's book is moving; read as a meditation upon the socially engaged spiritual life, it makes important and insightful contributions. His chapters on the Quaker peace testimony and on justice/ joyful witness offer a profound reconciliation of what may appear to be two irreconcilable forms of spiritually based social action: the prophetic stance, and the experiential encounter with the God of love. This is a spiritual path that faces evil but turns away from dehumanizing the evil-doer, that knows outrage but finally resides in gladness.

> —Sallie B. King, Professor of Religion, James
> Madison University, author of *Socially
> Engaged Buddhism* and *A Quaker's
> Response to Christian Fundamentalism*

CPSIA information can be obtained
at www.ICGtesting.com
Printed in the USA
FSOW02n1041250216
17277FS